MYSTICISM AND PROPHECY

MYSTICISM AND PROPHECY

The Dominican Tradition

RICHARD WOODS OP

SERIES EDITOR:
Philip Sheldrake

ORBIS BOOKS

Maryknoll, New York 10545

First published in 1998 by
Darton, Longman and Todd Ltd.
1 Spencer Court
140–142 Wandsworth High Street
London SW18 4JJ
Great Britain

Published in the USA in 1998 by
Orbis Books
P.O. Box 308
Maryknoll, New York 10545–0308
U.S.A.

Copyright © 1998 by Richard Woods

ISBN 1–57075–206–0

Designed by Sandie Boccacci
Phototypeset in 10/13¼pt New Century Schoolbook
by Intype London Ltd
Printed and bound in Great Britain by
Redwood Books, Trowbridge, Wiltshire

Library of Congress Cataloging-in-Publication Data

Woods, Richard, 1941–
    Mysticism and prophecy : the Dominican tradition / Richard Woods.
       p.   cm.—(Traditions of Christian spirituality)
    Includes bibliographical references and index.
    ISBN 1–57075–206–0 (pbk. : alk. paper)
    1. Dominicans—Spiritual life—History. I. Title. II. Series.
BX3503.W66 1998
255′.2—dc21
                                           98–19019
                                            CIP

CONTENTS

ACKNOWLEDGEMENTS

Thanks are due to the following for permission to quote copyright material:

Alba House, 2187 Victory Blvd., Staten Island, NY 10314–6603, for Giulana Cavallini, *Things Visible and Invisible: Images in the Spirituality of Catherine of Siena*, tr. Sr M. Jeremiah OP (New York: Alba House, 1996) and William Hinnebusch OP, *The History of the Dominican Order*, 2 vols. (Staten Island, NY: Alba House, Vol. 1 1966 and Vol. II 1973).

Paulist Press, 997 Macarthur Blvd., Mahwah, N 07430, for Joann Wolski Conn., *Spirituality and Personal Maturity* (New York: Paulist Press, 1989); Kevin W. Irwin, *Liturgy, Prayer and Spirituality* (New York: Paulist Press, 1984); Bonaventure, *The Soul's Journey into God* and other works, tr. and intro. by Ewart Cousins, preface by Ignatius Brady OFM (New York: Paulist Press, 1978); Catherine of Siena, *The Dialogue of Catherine of Siena*, tr. and ed. Suzanne Noffke OP (New York: Paulist Press, 1980); *Early Dominicans: Selected Writings*, ed. Simon Tugwell OP (New York: Paulist Press, 1982); Gregory of Nyssa, *The Life of Moses*, tr., intro., and notes by Everett Ferguson and Abraham J. Malherbe, preface by John Meyendorff (New York: Paulist Press, 1978); Henry Suso, *The Exemplar, with Two German Sermons*, tr. and ed. Frank Tobin, preface by Bernard McGinn (New York: Paulist Press, 1989); John Ruusbrocc, *The Spiritual Espousals and Other Works*, tr. and intro. by James Wiseman OSB, preface by Louis Dupré (New York: Paulist Press, 1985); *Pseudo-Dionysius: The Complete Works*, tr. Colm Luibheid, forward, notes and collaboration by Paul Rorem, preface by René Roques, and intro. by Jaroslav Pelikan, Jean Leclercq, and Karlfried Froelich (New York: Paulist Press, 1987); and Johann Tauler, *Sermons*, tr. Maria Shrady, intro. by Josef Schmidt, preface by Alois Haas (New York: Paulist Press, 1987).

Element Books Ltd, Shaftesbury, Dorset, for *Meister Eckhart, Sermons and Treatises*, tr. M. O'C. Walshe, 3 vols., 1987.

PREFACE TO THE SERIES

Nowadays, in the western world, there is a widespread hunger for spirituality in all its forms. This is not confined to traditional religious people, let alone to regular churchgoers. The desire for resources to sustain the spiritual quest has led many people to seek wisdom in unfamiliar places. Some have turned to cultures other than their own. The fascination with Native American or Aboriginal Australian spiritualities is a case in point. Other people have been attracted by the religions of India and Tibet or the Jewish Kabbalah and Sufi mysticism. One problem is that, in comparison to other religions, Christianity is not always associated in people's minds with 'spirituality'. The exceptions are a few figures from the past who have achieved almost cult status such as Hildegard of Bingen or Meister Eckhart. This is a great pity for Christianity East and West over two thousand years has given birth to an immense range of spiritual wisdom. Many traditions continue to be active today. Others that were forgotten are being rediscovered and reinterpreted.

It is a long time since an extended series of introductions to Christian spiritual traditions has been available in English. Given the present climate, it is an opportune moment for a new series which will help more people to be aware of the great spiritual riches available within the Christian tradition.

The overall purpose of the series is to make selected spiritual traditions available to a contemporary readership. The books seek to provide accurate and balanced historical and thematic treatments of their subjects. The authors are also conscious of the need to make connections with contemporary experience and values without being artificial or reducing a tradition to one dimension. The authors are well-versed in reliable scholarship about the traditions they describe. However, their intention is that the books should be fresh in style and accessible to the general reader.

One problem that such a series inevitably faces is the word 'spirituality'. For example, it is increasingly used beyond religious circles and does not necessarily imply a faith tradition. Again, it could mean substantially different things for a Christian and a Buddhist. Within Christianity itself, the word in its modern sense is relatively recent. The reality that it stands for differs subtly in the different contexts of time and place. Historically, 'spirituality' covers a breadth of human experience and a wide range of values and practices.

No single definition of 'spirituality' has been imposed on the authors in this series. Yet, despite the breadth of the series there is a sense of a common core in the writers themselves and in the traditions they describe. All Christian spiritual traditions have their source in three things. First, while drawing on ordinary experience and even religious insights from elsewhere, Christian spiritualities are rooted in the Scriptures and particularly in the Gospels. Second, spiritual traditions are not derived from abstract theory but from attempts to live out gospel values in a positive yet critical way within specific historical and cultural contexts. Third, the experiences and insights of individuals and groups are not isolated but are related to the wider Christian tradition of beliefs, practices and community life. From a Christian perspective, spirituality is not just concerned with prayer or even with narrowly religious activities. It concerns the whole of human life, viewed in terms of a conscious relationship with God, in Jesus Christ, through the indwelling of the Holy Spirit and within a community of believers.

The series as a whole includes traditions that probably would not have appeared twenty years ago. The authors themselves have been encouraged to challenge, where appropriate, inaccurate assumptions about their particular tradition. While conscious of their own biases, authors have none the less sought to correct the imbalances of the past. Previous understandings of what is mainstream or 'orthodox' sometimes need to be questioned. People or practices that became marginal demand to be re-examined. Studies of spirituality in the past frequently underestimated or ignored the role of women. Sometimes the treatments of spiritual traditions were culturally one-sided because they were written from an uncritical western European or North Atlantic perspective.

However, any series is necessarily selective. It cannot hope to do full justice to the extraordinary variety of Christian spiritual traditions. The principles of selection are inevitably open to question. I hope that an appropriate balance has been maintained between a sense of the likely readership on the one hand and the dangers of narrowness on the other. In the end, choices had to be made and the result is inevitably weighted in favour of traditions that have achieved 'classic' status or which seem to capture the contemporary imagination. Within these limits, I trust that the series will offer a reasonably balanced account of what the Christian spiritual tradition has to offer.

As editor of the series I would like to thank all the authors who agreed to contribute and for the stimulating conversations and correspondence that sometimes resulted. I am especially grateful for the high quality of their work which made my task so much easier. Editing such a series is a complex undertaking. I have worked closely throughout with Morag Reeve of Darton, Longman & Todd and Robert Ellsberg of Orbis Books. I am immensely grateful to them for their friendly support and judicious advice. Without them this series would never have come together.

Philip Sheldrake
Sarum College, Salisbury

INTRODUCTION: A RECONCILIATION OF OPPOSITES

Since the founding of the Order of Preachers in 1216, Dominican friars and sisters have contributed to Christian spirituality directly through teaching, writing, art, and not least, preaching. The first flowering of Dominican spirituality occurred in the thirteenth century and reached its heyday in the fourteenth, especially in Western Europe. Thomas Aquinas, Meister Eckhart, Catherine of Siena, Fra Angelico, Martin de Porres, Rose of Lima, and other saints and spiritual guides continue to inspire and influence women and men today throughout the world. Indirectly, Dominicans contributed to Christian spirituality through those they guided, inspired, and taught, including Ignatius of Loyola, Teresa of Ávila, Philip Neri and many other saints and spiritual leaders.

Attempting to provide a comprehensive account of the spirituality of the Order, even a large, multi-volume work, would require many years of patient textual research involving a vast range of information extending over almost 800 years and emanating from every part of the world.[1] In this comparatively brief work, I have chosen to present an interpretation based on a theme or pattern that in many respects polarizes, but neither defines nor circumscribes, the field of Dominican spirituality: the interplay of 'knowing' and 'unknowing' as elements in the broader dialectic of mystical contemplation and prophetic action.

Many aspects of Dominican spirituality do not fit comfortably within this framework, nor is it the particular property of the Order. Many non-Dominican spiritual figures, both Christian and non-Christian, have followed integrated pathways of mystical 'knowing unknowing' (*docta ignorantia*) and prophetic action.[2] Critical assessments of this kind or form of spirituality mention, among others, Philo, Augustine of Hippo, Dionysius the Areopagite, John Scottus (Eruigena), Ibn Arabi, Bonaventure, Marguerite Porete, the author of *The Cloud of Unknowing*, Nicholas of Cusa, Denis the Carthusian, and John of the Cross. Nevertheless, it seems to me that this configuration well characterizes the spirituality of the Order as a whole. Or, to put it slightly differently, those members of the Order recalled as outstanding embodiments of Dominican spirit manifest this approach to God in their lives and writings, particularly Thomas Aquinas, Meister Eckhart, and Catherine of Siena.

Even so, focusing on the interplay of the mystical and prophetic elements in the spiritualities of several outstanding Dominicans in the Middle Ages runs the considerable risk of misrepresentation, should the parts be taken for the whole. The narrower, if characteristic approach of Thomas Aquinas, Meister Eckhart, and Catherine of Siena, founded on the essential unknowability of God and the imperative of loving ministry, can be properly understood only in the context of the broader, richer spirituality of the Order and of the Church, the *kataphatic* (affirmative), richly sacramental, and artistically expressive dimensions of Christian spirituality. This is as it should be. Even Dionysius insisted that *apophatic* (negative) theology was a necessary counterpart in the threefold dialogue of positive, negative, and symbolic elements that constitute the dynamism of theology as a whole.

The subtext of my inquiry is less well-defined and, in fact, best left open: what is the potential of Dominican spirituality to transform lives and situations in the world today and, especially, tomorrow? More particularly, is the Dominican tradition, expressed in the lives and teaching of Thomas, Eckhart, and Catherine, as well as the other friars and sisters of the past, only a rich lode of historical data to be mined by textual scholars and biographers, or is it a series of guideposts for a way of life both meaningful and relevant to the present and the future?

Thus raising the question of the spirituality of the Dominican Order requires as well as complicates the discussion of its identity, purpose, and character. For 'spirituality' is itself a modern concept, not used in English before 1500 and in France only a short time before. In order to address the question adequately, it will be necessary to describe, at least briefly, what I mean by 'spirituality'.

WHAT IS SPIRITUALITY?

Recently, I was gently teased by a Dominican student who referred to spirituality as a field that doesn't exist. In fact, as a field of study, it not only exists, but represents one of the most vital and active areas of current academic research. Here, however, I am not especially concerned with spirituality as a field of study. Rather, I intend to explore Dominican spiritualities of knowing and 'unknowing' as ways of living that characterize an important aspect of what it means to be a member of the Order of Preachers and may also have value for persons outside the Order who are searching for spiritual guidance. Still, it is helpful to set out to some extent what we mean when we talk about spirituality in general, if only so the contours of *Dominican* spirituality will stand out in sharper relief.

Over the past several decades, spiritual writers and theologians have offered a number of serviceable descriptions of contemporary spirituality. The late Anglican theologian and writer, William Stringfellow, summed up many of these in his last, fine book, *The Politics of Spirituality*:

> ... whatever else may be affirmed about a spirituality which has biblical precedent and style, spiritual maturity or spiritual fulfillment necessarily involves the whole person – body, mind, soul, place, relationships – in connection with the whole of creation throughout the era of time.

> Biblical spirituality encompasses the whole person in the totality of existence in the world, not some fragment or scrap or incident of a person.[3]

More succinctly, Kenneth Leech wrote in his book, *Soul Friend*, 'the spiritual life is the life of the whole person directed toward God.'[4] In his excellent book on liturgy, prayer and spirituality, Kevin W. Irwin expands this notion helpfully:

> ... spirituality may be described as the experience of our relationship with God in faith and the ways in which we live out our faith. Spirituality involves our coming to know God, our response to God, and the prayer and work we perform in faith. For Christians, spirituality occurs in and among the community of the Church, the community formed by hearing and responding to the same call and invitation from God.[5]

Less formally, but with profound insight, Simon Tugwell observes that spirituality 'is not concerned with prayer and contemplation and spiritual exercises, it is concerned with people's ways of viewing things, the ways in which they try to make sense of the practicalities of christian living and to illuminate christian hopes and christian muddles.'[6]

Finally, for Joann Wolski Conn,

> The term spirituality refers to both a lived experience and an academic discipline. For Christians, it means one's entire life as understood, felt, imagined, and decided upon in relationship to God, in Christ Jesus, empowered by the Spirit. It also indicates the interdisciplinary study of this religious experience, including the attempt to promote its mature development.[7]

In the light of such a rich panorama of interpretations, I understand spirituality to be, first of all, from a biblical perspective, 'that in virtue of which a person is open to and transmits the life of God.'[8] Against a broader historical and social horizon, the term 'spirituality' also refers to the fund of beliefs, attitudes, values, practices of communities, Christian or otherwise, from which persons acquire and develop their personal identity and individual spiritualities. Third, as the biographically evident form of an individual's 'life journey', spirituality can be considered the product of a life-long interchange in which the radical capacity of a person to receive and transmit the gift of life is realized through concrete encounters in the natural and social world of her experience. Fourth, spirituality can also be considered as a field of study, which, like the study of religion or religious experience, is sometimes confused by its students with the object of their study – usually the second or third notions just mentioned. And these, the collective or communal forms of spirituality and the individual, unique form of a person's life-way, will be the focus of my attention in the following pages.

After Dominic himself, the representatives of the tradition who seem to me to reveal most clearly the genius and vitality of Dominican spirituality include Humbert of Romans, Albert the Great, Thomas Aquinas, Dietrich of Freiberg, Meister Eckhart, Henry Suso, John Tauler, Catherine of Siena, Vincent Ferrer, Jerome Savonarola, Catherine de' Ricci, Bartolomé de las Casas, Rose of Lima, Fra Angelico, John of St Thomas, Martin de Porres, Rose Hawthorn Lathrop, Henry Lacordaire, and closer to our own time, the biblical scholar Père Lagrange and Mary Joseph Rogers, who founded the Maryknoll Sisters. It is obviously impossible in a single work to consider all of them in depth. I hope that by concentrating chiefly on Thomas, Eckhart, and Catherine, who most clearly seem to embody what I perceive to be the outstanding features of Dominican spirituality in its original scholarly, mystical, and prophetic expression, the lives and contributions of their many sisters and brothers will also stand out in sharper relief.

I remain especially indebted to the patient research and thoughtful reflections of my Dominican associates and friends, teachers and preachers all, Benedict Ashley, Brian Davies, Suzanne Noffke, Simon Tugwell, and the late James Weisheipl, to whom this book is affectionately dedicated.

1. THE DOMINICAN ORDER AND ITS SPIRITUAL TRADITION

Since the founding of the Order of Preachers in the early thirteenth century, many Dominicans have been recognized as eminent spiritual teachers, writers, and guides as well as saints. Nevertheless, it would be mistaken to presume either that there is such a thing as 'a' Dominican spirituality which is somehow adequately differentiated from Carmelite, Franciscan, Jesuit, and other forms of Christian spirituality, or, more to the point, that there is some overarching spiritual doctrine under whose flag all Dominican ships sail.[1] On one hand, there are a variety of spiritualities *within* the Dominican tradition, some strikingly different from others. In the 782 years of its history, thousands of preachers, theologians, philosophers, missionaries, reformers, healers, scientists, historians, painters, sculptors, musicians, and writers have embodied the spirit of the Order, each contributing to and drawing from its spirituality in distinctive ways. On the other hand, there is considerable overlap between the spiritualities of the Order of Preachers and those of other orders and congregations and even entire traditions.

Yet, far from asserting that there are only the discrete spiritualities of a motley tribe of individuals all of whom identify themselves as Dominican, or some generic spirituality that covers a multitude of groupings, it seems to me that there are several specific elements or attributes that characterize the friars and sisters of the Order of Preachers individually and collectively. Although there is no foundational work like the *Spiritual Exercises* of St Ignatius, or even the *Little Flowers of St Francis*, that comprehensively emblematizes Dominican spirituality, it would be off the mark to assume that either anarchy or diffuseness prevails.

THE EARLY DOMINICANS AND THE DOMINICAN FAMILY TODAY

The first Preachers were male. But women had played an important role in the preaching mission of Diego and Dominic from the beginning. In many respects, the establishment of the convent of nuns at Prouille as a refuge for women converted from the Albigensian heresy was the first 'Dominican' foundation. In any event, Dominic soon founded other monasteries for nuns, and the 'Sisters Preachers' were fully incorporated into the Order in 1267. While under the spiritual authority of the Master of the Order, however, the women remain independent of the friars. This is also true of the great number of non-cloistered Dominican congregations of sisters throughout the world. And while the friars have remained largely clerical in that, like the canons from which they arose, most of the members are eventually ordained to the priesthood, non-clerical co-operator brothers share full membership in the Order. Lay persons dedicated to the spirituality of the Order and following their own rule, including both married and single persons living as ordinary citizens in society, complete the Dominican Family.

DOMINICAN SPIRITUALITY: A PLURALITY OF RESOURCES

In the beginning, less attention was paid to defining what made the Friars and Sisters Preachers different from everyone else than to identify what made them what they were: their mission. In the papal letter of Honorius III to Dominic and the first friars in 1216, the pope described the purpose of the Order with remarkable simplicity: ' . . . a life of poverty and regular observance and . . . preaching the Word of God and proclaiming the name of our Lord Jesus Christ throughout the world.'[2] As

Bede Jarrett put it, the early friars 'took as their boast what [the Benedictine chronicler] Matthew of Paris used to say of them with scorn: "That the whole world was their cell and the ocean was their cloister." '[3]

According to the prologue of the earliest Constitutions, the Order 'is known from the beginning to have been instituted especially for preaching and the salvation of souls.' Citing these words, the present Constitutions continue, 'Our brethren, therefore, according to the command of the founder "must conduct themselves honorably and religiously as men who want to obtain their salvation and the salvation of others, following in the footsteps of the Savior as evangelical men speaking among themselves or their neighbors either with God or about God"' (*Primitive Const.*, Dist II, c. 31).

The distinctive character of the Order is aptly summarized in the following paragraph from the Constitutions (Section IV):

> We also undertake as sharers of the apostolic mission the life of the Apostles in the form conceived by St Dominic, living with one mind the common life, faithful in the profession of the evangelical counsels, fervent in the common celebration of the liturgy, especially of the Eucharist and the divine office as well as other prayer, assiduous study, and persevering in regular observance. All these practices contribute not only to the glory of God and our sanctification, but serve directly the salvation of humankind, since they prepare harmoniously for preaching, furnish its incentive, form its character, and in turn are influenced by it. These elements are closely interconnected and carefully balanced, mutually enriching one another, so that in their synthesis the proper life of the Order is established: a life in the fullest sense apostolic, in which preaching and teaching must proceed from an abundance of contemplation.

William Hinnebusch, one of the most distinguished recent historians of the Order, has persuasively argued that the character of the Order and therefore its spirituality are rooted

in its origins as an order of Canons Regular, priests assigned
to a cathedral living in common and following a monastic rule.
St Dominic was, we know, a Canon Regular at the Cathedral
of Osma, where the community followed the Rule of St Augustine. It is a logical, but often ignored, consequence that when
Dominic decided to establish an order of preaching friars, he
modelled it on what he knew. Hinnebusch points out that

> The bull of confirmation issued by Pope Honorius III on
> December 22, 1216 began with the words *Religiosam
> vitam*. Hundreds of similar bulls open with the same
> words and with the same general content. They vary in
> detail but are always given in favor of chapters of canons
> regular. The chief duty of the canons was contemplative –
> the worship of the Holy Trinity. The canons existed in
> order to carry out the divine worship of the Church in a
> solemn manner.[4]

Canons had other duties, of course, and despite the monastic
features of their life, they were not monks. Nevertheless a
liturgically-focused life of contemplation was specifically their
calling. And, in due course, 'The issuance of the [bull] *Reli-
giosam vitam* by Pope Honorius served notice on the Friars
Preachers that they were Canons Regular and that their chief
function was to worship God in a contemplative way.'[5]

Contemporaries of the early friars were aware of this
character of their life. Lester Little cites the testimony to
this effect by one of the keenest observers of religious move-
ments in the thirteenth century, Bishop Jacques de Vitry:

> In the *Histories of the East and of the West*, written in the
> early 1220s, [de Vitry] devoted a chapter to the Domini-
> cans at Bologna, although never calling them by their
> official name. He saw them as a house of canons, observing
> the canonical hours and otherwise living in conformity
> with the Rule of St Augustine. At the same time he was
> fully aware of their exceptional qualities. Completely
> willing to follow naked the naked Christ, they treated

all material things and all worldly matters as so much excrement; they accepted alms, he said, but for the present day only never giving any thought to the future. They taught and studied at the university and on feast days they preached, in accordance with a special commission given by the Roman pontiff. They have fused an order of preachers to an order of canons. This felicitous mixture of good elements attracts, stimulates, and fires up a great many people to follow them; each day this holy and distinguished congregation of Christ's students both grows in number and expands in charity.'[6]

Hinnebusch concludes that the spirituality of the Friars Preachers, as fundamentally a group of canons, is

theocentric, Christological, sacerdotal . . . monastic, contemplative, and apostolic. It is, in truth, the spirituality of Christ the Preacher and of the Apostles. The primary intention is to elevate the friar to the heights of contemplation, but going beyond this, the Dominican contemplation itself is intended to fructify in the apostolate for souls, especially through preaching, teaching, and writing. Contemplation is the generic element, the one the Friars Preachers share with other contemplative Orders, the salvation of souls through preaching is the specific note distinguishing Dominicans from all other Orders.[7]

Using a more functional rather than structural approach, in his recent short history of the Order, Benedict Ashley identifies four fundamental characteristics of Dominican spirituality. First, the mission of the Order of Preachers is evangelization – spreading the gospel of Christ, the good news of the Reign of God, specifically by *preaching*. Significantly, evangelical preaching is 'a communitarian work and hence primarily the responsibility of the whole community.'[8] Dominican life and spirituality are, therefore, fundamentally *communal*. Third, *worship and prayer* are primary expressions of that communal identity.

Dominic retained the monastic liturgy of the Hours and community Eucharist (which modern communities were to privatize in order to free themselves more for their work), although he was willing to dispense brethren from attendance at every service in view of study or preaching. Preaching must flow from contemplation of the Divine Word to be preached and this is most perfectly expressed in community worship based as it is on meditation on the Bible and the commemoration of the great saving events of Christ's life and their imitation by the saints.[9]

Spiritual discipline or 'ascetical' practice is an important aspect of Dominican spirituality, and chief among its elements, historically, has been the observance of evangelical poverty, the voluntary renunciation of private property.[10] Even more central was the replacement of manual labour by *study*, especially of Scripture, as a personal commitment and spiritual discipline specifically characteristic of the Order. Of significant consequence for the Church as a whole, according to William Hinnebusch, was that with this innovation, 'for the first time in a thousand years of monastic history, a religious Order incorporated into its rule sections dealing with the academic life.'[11]

Thus, for Ashley,

These four elements ... sum up Dominican spirituality: *(1) Dominican spirituality is a share in Jesus Christ the Word in his mission of announcing the Good News of salvation which he himself is; (2) This calling is fulfilled by a community out of its experience of living for God and for neighbors; (3) The source of its light is prayer, especially liturgical prayer, for which one is freed by ascetic discipline and simplicity of life; (4) This prayer is fed by assiduous study of the Scriptures and of all sources of truth that help us to understand the Word of God.*[12]

Historically, the iconography of the Order is instructive in its own way. The original 'coat of arms' found on Dominican seals, stationery, books, documents, inscriptions, and paintings portrays a central white triangle surmounted by two black sections representing the habit and mantle or cloak of the members. Ordinarily emblazoned on a banner surrounding the shield are the Latin words *Laudare, Benedicere, Praedicare*: 'to Praise, to Bless, to Preach'. This threefold Latin motto points to the main elements of our life, our mission, and therefore our spirituality: prayer and worship, particularly the communal celebration of the Liturgy of the Church; evangelical ministry, expressed in sacramental administration, missionary work, teaching, healing, parochial care; and above all else, preaching in its many forms, including writing and the expressive arts.

Similarly, the single word *Veritas*, 'Truth', often inscribed over the Dominican seal, summarizes in its own way the goal and ideal of the Order. By this is meant not some narrow, philosophical, much less semantic, notion of verbal accuracy, but the whole range of divine, physical, and human Reality. Thomas Aquinas would write three volumes on the meaning of truth in this light, but for him, as for all Dominicans, the chief instance and perfect exemplar remains Eternal Truth, expressed substantially and historically in Jesus Christ: 'In other men we find many participated truths, insofar as the First Truth gleams back into their minds through many likenesses; but Christ is Truth itself. Thus it is said: "In whom all the treasures of wisdom are hidden" (Col. 2:3).'[13]

Still another epithet has served to illustrate the spirituality of the Order and its members: *Contemplata aliis Tradere*, 'to hand on to others what has been contemplated.' Drawn from the teachings of St Thomas Aquinas,[14] this gnomic phrase is meant not to distinguish the mystical, contemplative dimension of Dominican spirituality from its active expression, but to unite them. Nor are they related as a means to an end: they form one goal.

Synoptically, then, the characteristic themes found in Dominican spirituality will generally include the following:

The constitutive priorities of preaching, community life,
prayer, and study
Poverty of Spirit
The primacy of Truth
Contemplation expressed in Active Ministry

To these may be added, I suggest, the quest for ever-closer
union with God, the unknowable Source and Goal of our being,
life, and consciousness, through conformity to Christ under
the influence of the gifts of the Holy Spirit. This, the mystical
core of our spirituality, is not limited to Dominicans, of course,
but as studied by generations of teachers in our tradition,
especially characterizes the lives of our greatest saints.[15]

THE WAYLESS WAY: A TRADITION WITHOUT A METHOD

The character of Dominican preaching down through the centuries, and therefore of Dominican life and spirituality, is
perhaps most accurately if somewhat dangerously described
as doctrinal. That is not to say it is erudite, although it may be.
Or that it is dogmatic, which it often is, not to say sometimes
regrettably apodictic in expression. But it is based on the
sovereign role of Truth in the life of the Christian and the
Church. For Dominicans, teaching and preaching are not two
different functions or works, but two aspects of the same work,
two sides of a single coin. To the extent that our preaching is
not founded on the study of Divine Truth in Scripture and the
book of the world, it is not Dominican, nor is our teaching, to
the extent that it is not the expression of that same Truth.

One of the earliest Dominican treatises that is clearly 'spiritual' in the sense with which we are familiar today is the *Talks
of Instruction* by Meister Eckhart, which emanate from the
turn of the fourteenth century.[16] In these instructions, given
by Eckhart when he was prior of the community at Erfurt,
most likely to the novices and junior members of the priory,
not only did he expound creatively on the ordinary religious

life of the Preaching Friars, but in many respects anticipated his own, more mature doctrine that would unfold over the next two decades and more in over a hundred sermons and treatises. Here, as in his later works, Eckhart espouses a characteristic thirteenth-century approach, avoiding talk about 'experiences', 'practices', and the like, concentrating instead on principles and interpretation. In the *Talks*, Eckhart already regards particular 'ways' of devotion with suspicion, intending to instil a more general attitude, particularly what he calls 'detachment', *abegesheidenheit*, in his students rather than attempting to 'form' them according to some predefined spiritual practice.

In the end, ours is a spirituality *characteristically* without a method, or a technique, or a favoured set of exercises. It is founded on our mission, and that mission is the same as it was in the beginning: to announce the good news of salvation, the acceptable day of the Lord. Today and tomorrow, as well as through the centuries behind us, Dominicans are simply preachers, or they are nothing at all.

2. DOMINIC AND THE EARLY PREACHERS

When the bishops of the Second Vatican Council urged members of religious orders to return to the spirit of their founders,[1] they were alluding to the belief that the character and destiny of entire institutes were foreshadowed in the personality and teachings of those men and women who initiated what are in most cases now centuries-old organizations. There is truth in that belief, as there is in all mythic statement. Yet there is also a tendency of later generations to read back into the character and circumstances of originating figures such as Benedict, Francis, and Dominic what was in fact the gradual development of the charism of the orders they founded. As a consequence, historical judgement can sometimes strike us as disconcerting, if not disenchanting, when it fails to discover evident seeds of the present in those revered figures of the past. It need not, insofar as the spirit of a religious tradition grows and develops as truly as does any living organism. The character it manifests in time is the product of its successes and failures in meeting the demands of history. And that is why it sometimes becomes necessary to look back, if only to reassure ourselves that oaks do not betray acorns, but fulfil them.

THE CANON FROM CASTILLE

Dominic was born in the town of Caleruega in central Spain around the year 1170. His parents, Felix and Juana (or Joanna) were members of the nobility.[2] His birth and childhood have been endowed by later biographers with incidents commonly ascribed to future saints, but it is clear enough that he was possessed of profound spiritual gifts from an early age.[3]

Marked for a career in the Church, Dominic was first educated by an uncle who was a priest, then sent to the university at Palencia until 1194. Returning to Osma, the local cathedral city, he was ordained and became a canon there under the reforming bishop, Martin de Bazan, and his astute, energetic prior, Diego de Acabes. Soon, Diego succeeded Martin as bishop. By then, Dominic was already subprior. There was a strong affinity between the two men, one based not least on their passion for ministry to the poor and ignorant.

When in 1203 Diego was dispatched by King Alfonso VIII on a diplomatic mission to Sweden, his choice of a companion fell on Dominic. As they travelled to the lands of the north, they passed through southern France, the Midi, where Albigensian Cathars, Waldensians, and other heterodox sects vied with orthodox Christians for the loyalty of the people. By the time Diego and Dominic returned to Sweden in 1205, Pope Innocent III had launched a preaching campaign against the heretics under the supervision of a number of Cistercian abbots. Already fired with thoughts of returning to the borders of Christendom as missionaries, the two Spaniards met the dispirited legates as they returned to Osma.

Having failed to impress the austere and sincere Albigensians, for whom apostolic simplicity and poverty were essential emblems of holiness, the monks turned to Diego for advice. Diego not only told them that the wealth and ostentation of their entourage undermined their message, but when pressed to provide leadership, he undertook to provide an example, sending away his horses, fine clothing, and retinue. Soon, Diego and Dominic were effectively leading the preaching mission.

By the end of 1206, the Spaniards had succeeded in establishing a monastery for women converts at Prouille, near the heretical stronghold of Fanjeaux. Modelled on the apostolic houses of the Albigensians, the convent provided a base of

operation as well as a refuge for women who would have otherwise been resourceless.[4]

Later that year, Diego returned to Osma, leaving Dominic
in charge of the mission. But within a few months, the bishop
had returned and engaged, alongside Dominic, in two weeks
of debate with Albigensian leaders at Montpellier. Despite
success in argument, the mission eventually collapsed with
the death of one and departure of the second of the three most
prominent Cistercian legates. Then, at the end of December,
Diego himself died in Osma. Finally, early in 1208, the third
legate, Pierre of Castelnau, was assassinated. The preaching
mission was soon replaced by an armed crusade.

Dominic continued his preaching work and, although he
became a friend of the leader of the crusade, Simon de
Montfort, he disengaged himself from the military conquest of
the Midi.[5] His preaching met with little success, however. He
seems to have made only two converts during the next six
years, one of whom, Roger Pons, relapsed in 1215.

But the germ of an idea was maturing in Dominic's mind.
As Diego had seen so clearly, the only hope of ever succeeding
was for the preachers to surpass the evangelical simplicity and
dedication of the heretics by a wholly new form of life. In Fulk,
the Bishop of Toulouse, Dominic found a new ally and friend.
In 1214, the bishop gave Dominic care of a parish in Fanjeaux.
Within the year, the new papal legate, Peter of Benevento,
appointed Dominic the head of the preaching mission with
headquarters in Toulouse. By the summer of 1215, Dominic
had attracted his first recruits. In 1216, he travelled with Fulk
to Rome to begin the process of winning confirmation of what
would become the first Order of Preachers, a community of
brothers and sisters committed to an apostolic life of radical
poverty, simplicity, learning, and missionary zeal.

Following the death of Innocent III in 1216, a series of papal
bulls issued by his successor, Honorius III, established the
band of apostolic preachers in Toulouse. But Dominic's vision
of a larger, indeed worldwide Order continued to develop, not
without opposition and interior struggles.[6] Dominic himself

lived only five more years, dying in Bologna on 6 August 1221, exhausted and ill from constant travel, preaching, and the demands of guiding and nurturing the infant communities of both friars and nuns.

Clamour for his canonization began at once. Although resisted at first by the friars, fearing distraction from the mission Dominic had bequeathed them, the process gathered momentum. Many eye-witnesses submitted testimony regarding his life, holiness, and miracles, culminating in Dominic's formal enrolment among the saints of God on 3 July 1234, by his old friend at the papal court, Cardinal Hugolino, once protector of the Order and now Pope Gregory IX.[7] By then, the Order had spread to every country in Europe, and Saint Dominic's popularity loomed large among all classes of people, becoming the matter even of troubadour ballads.

DOMINIC AND HIS SPIRITUALITY

Physically, despite later portraits of Dominic as being dark of hair and eye, he was fair, possibly because of Gothic ancestry. Most likely, as in the case of his later compatriot, Ignatius of Loyola, he was blue-eyed. According to the deposition of Sister Cecelia, one of the nuns who remembered Dominic well,

> He was of medium height: his figure supple, his face handsome and slightly sanguine, his hair and beard blond with a slight reddish tinge, his eyes beautiful. From his brow and eyes there emanated a certain radiant splendor which won the admiration and veneration of all. He always appeared joyous and smiling except when moved with compassion at some affliction of his neighbor. His hands were long and handsome and his powerful voice noble and sonorous. He was not in the least bald and wore the religious tonsure entire, sprinkled with a few white hairs.[8]

We know little of Dominic's 'interior' life from his own words, for he rarely spoke of himself at all. Contemporaries like Cecelia remembered him as cheerful and energetic, sometimes given to a certain effervescence if not flamboyance of character. On one occasion, he learned that he had been targeted for assassination by some Albigensians (who did in fact murder one of the original legates, Pierre of Castelnau, in 1208, and in 1252 also killed the first Dominican martyr, Peter of Verona). Rather than take evasive action, as one of the would-be assassins himself later testified, Dominic went past the danger zone singing at the top of his lungs.

From other accounts, it appears that Dominic liked to sing and did so frequently (and loudly) on his many trips through Spain, France, and Italy. Not a man to stifle his feelings, witnesses testified after his death that Dominic was noisy at prayer as well, often in his later years awakening the brethren from the chapel with his roars and groans. One somewhat comic result was a notation in the customary drawn up at the first chapter of the Order in 1220 advising novice masters to instruct the novices on how to pray quietly.[9]

Dominic was often moved to tears by the plight of orthodox Christians, heretics, and pagans, so many of whom seemed to him to be lost sheep desperately seeking a good shepherd. His life-long goal was to become a missionary to the fierce barbarian tribes of the North-East, an ambition cut short by his untimely death just over the age of fifty.

Already committed to an austere and simple form of life as a young canon at Osma, throughout his life Dominic avoided even simple comforts when he could and adopted many of the ascetical practices associated with the reform movement favoured by Martin de Bazan and Diego. He fasted frequently and abstained from meat entirely. Alone in the chapel at night, he scourged himself on behalf of 'poor sinners'. Committed wholly to evangelical poverty, he possessed only a single habit, refused to carry money, and would not allow anyone so much as to carry his shoes for him.[10]

Although from his youth Dominic's love of books and learning was famous, he was not an academic. One of the most telling of the accounts of his student years concerns a wrenching decision he made while at Palencia to sell his beloved (and expensive) books to buy bread for the poor during a famine. 'I refuse to study dead skins while men are dying of hunger,' he was reported to have said, according to the deposition of Bro. Stephen, the Provincial of Lombardy at the time of the canonization process. One of the first to join the band of preachers, Stephen said he heard the story from 'reliable people' before he met Dominic. Stephen also pointed out that other scholars followed Dominic's example.[11]

Study remained important to Dominic, especially in the early days of the preachers at the church of St Romain in Toulouse, when he secured the services of an English scholar, Alexander of Stavensby, to lecture the new recruits on Scripture. Unable to obtain teachers from Paris, in 1217 Dominic sent some of the new preachers there for training. Less than a year later, he began a house in Bologna, home of the second great European university.[12]

For Dominic and his followers, study was a means to an end. The primary goal always remained preaching. But preaching well, Dominic firmly believed, required understanding. Thus, the first houses of the new Order were usually established near centres of learning, generally the great universities.[13] By 1221, friars had arrived at Oxford. A generation later, when the exciting ideas of the mystical theology of Dionysius penetrated to Paris, Cologne, and elsewhere, along with other daring new imports, it is hardly surprising that the Preaching Friars found themselves among the most attentive students.

EARLY DOMINICAN SPIRITUALITY

Raymond Martin claimed that 'Saint Dominic was a mystic, "the equal of the great mystics"; by his wise legislation, he laid the enduring foundations of an organization with a mystical life which has lived and developed throughout the centuries.'[14] Such a view is not contradicted by Simon Tugwell's observation that

... the early Dominicans were not particularly concerned,

either for themselves or for others, with what has come to be called the 'interior life.' Some of them, certainly, were great men of prayer, but their prayer was simple, devotional, and largely petitionary. But there is no hint of any methodical 'mental prayer,' such as we find in later centuries, nor is there any sign of any theory of mystical progress attached to these simple prayers. When thirteenth-century Dominicans do comment on the ascent of the soul to God, it is in intellectualist terms that belong more within the domain of speculative theology than in the kind of mystical theology we have since become used to.[15]

It can safely be said that the spirituality of the Dominican Order, in all its branches, reflects the spirit and intentions of St Dominic even though some of its features, had he been able to foresee them, might have startled that exuberant Spaniard as it grew to its present extent. Above all, Dominic was a man of prayer who utilized the full resources of the learning available to him to preach, to teach, and even materially to assist those searching for the truth found in the gospel of Christ. It is that spirit which he bequeathed to his followers.

DOMINIC'S SUCCESSORS

In addition to the personality of Dominic himself and the legislation of the early chapters, the formative influences on the spirituality of the early friars and sisters were, as the saying goes, many and varied. The rising tide of new ideas, academic controversies, and even the new urban environment in which the friars exercised their ministry played a determinative role. But charismatic leaders such as Blessed Jordan of Saxony, Dominic's successor as Master, Reginald of Orleans, and Hugh of St Cher, left a lasting impression. Outstanding among this 'second generation' of friars were Dominic's fifth successor as Master, Humbert of Romans, and the great scholar and master of Thomas Aquinas and Eckhart, Albert of Lauingen.

Master of Preachers

Humbert of Romans, Master from 1254 to 1263, deeply affected the Order by the soundness and perspicacity of his administrative decisions as well as by his preaching and writing, even after his resignation. Guiding the Order during some of the most dangerous years of its early history, Humbert's organizational genius and pastoral sensibility left its stamp in almost every area of Dominican life, not least in liturgy and formation. He secured the recognition of the sisters as integral members of the Order. Humbert also particularly encouraged the study of languages, especially Arabic, in view of the missionary work to which the friars were increasingly committed in the East. But an emphasis on developing excellence in preaching was his most enduring legacy, the formation of the spirituality of young preachers his constant concern.

Born around 1200 at Romans, near Valence in southern France, Humbert first studied at the University of Paris. After becoming Master of Arts, he stayed on to study canon law and theology. Although he had once considered becoming a Carthusian, towards the end of 1224 he entered the Order at Paris. Within two years, he was lecturing in theology at Lyons. By 1237 he was elected prior there, and within a year he was elected provincial of the province of Rome. In 1244 or 1245 he was elected Provincial of France. In 1254 he was elected Master at the General Chapter held in Buda at the invitation of King Bela IV of Hungary.[16]

During Humbert's tenure as Master, the most serious attack against the mendicant Orders was launched in 1254 by the secular masters at the University of Paris. Thomas Aquinas was at the centre of much of the controversy, and Humbert worked tirelessly and eventually successfully in Rome to secure the privileges of the Dominicans and Franciscans.

In 1263 at the General Chapter in London, Humbert resigned as master, probably for reasons of health. Offered the Patriarchate of Jerusalem, he refused, and returned to Lyons, where he devoted the remaining fourteen years of his life chiefly to writing. Death came on 14 July 1277. The following year, Humbert's name was officially inscribed in the Martyrology of the Order. He was, as Bernard Gui wrote early in the next century, 'prudent, circumspect, learned, and, above all the men of this generation, aglow with God's grace.' But, despite his reputation for sanctity, and although venerated within the Order, he was never beatified.

Works

Humbert contributed a considerable and varied body of writings to the Order and the Church. One of his projects as master was to organize and supervise the preparation of liturgical books. He also collected information about the earliest days of the Order and the lives of Dominic and the first Dominicans. He wrote a *Letter on Regular Observance*, a commentary on the Rule of St Augustine, and a letter dealing with various problems that had arisen about Dominican legislation.

Considered the most productive author of the thirteenth century of works on preaching, Humbert wrote three important books, *On the Gift of Fear*, the beginning of an unfinished book on the gifts of the Holy Spirit, a handbook of sermons for preachers of the Crusade, and a remarkable instruction on *The Formation of Preachers*, a compendium of sketches or models of sermons for a wide range of people, circumstances, and occasions, from pilgrimages and funerals to major feast days.

Finally, in preparation for the Council of Lyons, probably at the request of the next Master of the Order, he wrote the *Opus Tripartitum*, which examines the question of a new Crusade, the reunion of the Eastern and Western Churches, relations between the Greeks and the Latins, and various issues regarding the reform of the Latin Church.

Spirituality

Although not primarily remembered for his contributions to the spirituality of the Order, Humbert, Fr Martin remarks, 'added spiritual works of the highest importance, whose content was within the reach of even the weakest. A perfect oralist, endowed with remarkable religious good sense, using clear, simple language wherein anecdotes and examples abound, he stands at the heart of the ascetic writers of the order.'[17]

Among his spiritual counsels for enthusiastic young Dominicans is found this prudent advice,

> They are also to be instructed not to be eager to see visions or work miracles, since these avail little to salvation, and sometimes we are fooled by them; but rather they should be eager to do good in which salvation consists. Also, they should be taught not to be sad if they do not enjoy the divine consolations they hear others have; but they should know the loving Father for some reason sometimes withholds these. Again, they should learn that if they lack the grace of compunction or devotion they should not think they are not in the state of grace as long as they have good will which is all that God regards.[18]

Leader of Leaders

Evaluating the contribution of this multi-faceted man, Raymond Hinnebusch wrote,

> Humbert of Romans was one of the finest men produced by the Dominican Order; in turn, he was like Jordan [of Saxony] one of those who did most to crystallize the Dominican character. An inspired preacher and the experienced occupant of major offices in the Order, Humbert enjoyed the confidence of a series of popes, of the college of cardinals, and of King Louis IX of France.[19]

In regularizing the formation of young Dominicans and defending its scholars, Humbert was aided and, in turn, supported two of the brightest stars in the Dominican array, Thomas Aquinas and that remarkable German who taught Thomas and, of all the stellar personalities of the period, alone is honoured as 'Great'.

Great Albert

Albert's impression on the intellectual and spiritual character of the Order is deep and indelible. An astonishingly erudite figure, he was pre-eminent as a scientist, philosopher, theologian, spiritual writer, ecumenist, diplomat, and saint, known even in his own lifetime as Magnus, 'the Great'. Under the aegis of Humbert of Romans, Albert helped reshape the curriculum of studies for all Dominican students, introduced the study of Aristotle, and explored the depths of Neoplatonic philosophy and mysticism.

A Wonderful Life

Born in Lauingen on the Danube about 1200, Albert first studied natural science at the University of Padua.[20] Attracted to the Order by the magnetic appeal of Jordan of Saxony in 1223, he was sent to Bologna for additional studies, then on to Paris, where he became Master in Theology.

Despite the suspicion and hostility of many of the Paris masters and powerful church leaders towards the newly-discovered works of Aristotle coming into vogue at the university, Albert quickly recognized their value and began a series of commentaries on the major books. He also became deeply interested in the Neoplatonist writings of the late classical era, including the Christian works of Dionysius, that were being newly translated into Latin.

As a leading light at the University of Paris, he noticed then nurtured the budding genius of the young Thomas, who accompanied him to Cologne for further studies when Albert began a new centre of study there in 1248. He was elected German provincial, and in 1260 accepted the office of Bishop of Ratisbon despite the urgent pleas of Humbert. A year later, he resigned and returned to teaching and writing. His literary output was prodigious, although Albert's hope of producing a great *Summa Theologiae* was never realized. Still active in his mid-seventies, he mounted a vigorous defence of the rights of the mendicants to teach at the University of Paris and defended the orthodoxy of his great pupil, Thomas.

By the end of his long life, Albert had shaped two more generations of teachers and writers, including to some extent the greatest preacher and mystical writer of the fourteenth century, Eckhart of Hochheim. After a long and productive life, he died in Cologne in 1280.

Albert's Writings

Among Albert's voluminous works, there is a valuable commentary on the *Divine Names* of 'Dionysius the Areopagite', that mysterious figure whose mystical theology would exercise such a lasting influence on the Middle Ages and beyond.[21] Albert was not the first Dominican to address himself to Dionysius. Bartholomew of Breganza, received as a novice by St Dominic, later regent master of theology in the papal palace, and eventually bishop, wrote two works on Dionysian themes. But as the only scholar of the thirteenth century to comment on the whole corpus, Albert's attention is surely a large part of the reason why Dionysius grew in importance as a major theological resource in the later Middle Ages.

A scientist and philosopher of note, Albert's theological and spiritual writings contributed significantly to the growth of the German mystical movement already in full bloom among Beguines and nuns in the tradition of Hildegard of Bingen and Albert's close contemporary, Mechthild of Magdeburg. (Mechthild had many Dominican ties. Her brother Baldwin was a member of the Order and one of Albert's students, Henry of Halle, was her confessor and early editor of her great book, *The Flowing Light of the Godhead*.)

Albert's Spirituality

Thomas of Cantimprè, a student of Albert's and a biographer of several saints, including his master, described how even as Regent Master Albert devoted himself to prayer day and night, reciting the entire psalter daily. Thomas is echoed by William of Tocco, who in his deposition regarding Thomas reminds us of Albert that 'this wonderful master offered his students simultaneously the knowledge of wisdom and the example of a holy life.'[22]

Hinnebusch writes,

> Albert's writings manifest his own genuine mystical personality and sensitivity. In them he consistently interlarded spiritual doctrine with theological speculation, especially in his [unfinished] *Summa Theologiae* and commentaries on the Scriptures and Pseudo-Dionysius. As Grabmann points out, it is sufficient to read the Prologue to Albert's Summa to discover his personal inclination toward mysticism. Many passages in his exegetical works express ideas, reveal attitudes of surrender to God, and show his love for the Savior and the Virgin Mother.[23]

Teaching

Albert's works have received less attention than they merit despite the resurgence in medieval studies during the last century. Reasons for this are mixed – the overwhelming brilliance of his greatest student, the incomparable Thomas Aquinas, but also the daring brightness of Eckhart, Suso, and Tauler; and, even more recently, interest in the works of Dietrich of Freiberg and other members of Albert's school. And although Albert was a pioneer in integrating Aristotle into the framework of Christian thought, he was much more open to

Neoplatonist sources than many Catholic (and Protestant) scholars have found comfortable.

As might be expected from someone drawn to the mystical theology of the ancient Church, especially that of Dionysius, Albert espoused the dialectic of positive and negative elements that, as we shall see, are so characteristic of that approach to the knowledge of God:

> negative ways of doing theology begin . . . by taking what is clear to us and perceptible to our senses and denying it of God. They proceed in this way, separating everything from God, so that our understanding is left with something unclear, from which all that it knows has been taken away and about which it cannot say what it is. Affirmative ways of doing theology, on the other hand, bring the hidden- ness of the Godhead out into the open, inasmuch as they indicate how the things that are manifest to us proceed from a transcendent cause. For example, when God is called 'good' this signifies that he is the one from whom all goodness in creatures is derived, and when he is called 'Father' this means that he is the one 'from whom all fatherhood in heaven and on earth is named.'[24]

Albert follows Dionysius, holding that positive knowledge of God is possible, but obscure. We are on more certain ground in knowing what God is not:

> . . . we affirm things of God only relatively, that is, causally, whereas we deny things of God absolutely, that is, with reference to what he is in himself. And there is no contra- diction between a relative affirmation and an absolute negation. It is not contradictory to say that someone is white-toothed and not white.[25]

Other themes that will appear in sharper focus in Thomas are found first in Albert. Hinnebusch points out that

> . . . Albert was the first theologian to explain how the gifts of wisdom and understanding perfect the virtues of faith

and are the organs of God's direct intervention in the act of contemplation. Infused wisdom, an affective knowledge of God, is caused by love in the soul but also increases love. Contemplation is mediate; the mind by reference to abstract species strips finite qualities of their imperfections to reach toward the infinite, but it knows only that God is (*Quia est*) not what he is (*Quid est*). Contemplation always remains a 'confused' knowledge of God; through it the soul sees God in the sense that it is elevated above created being, but it does not see Him in himself.[26]

In Albert's Wake

If, among Albert's disciples, Thomas and Eckhart became the most brilliant luminaries of the Order and indeed of much of Europe in the thirteenth and early fourteenth centuries, they were by no means solitary stars. Among Albert's other notable students were John and Gerald Korngin of Sterngassen, Dietrich of Freiberg, Ulrich Englebert of Strassburg, Berthold of Moosburg, and Henry of Halle. [27] Ulrich, Dietrich, and Berthold, like Eckhart after them, became known for carrying further Albert's enthusiasm for Neoplatonism and mystical spirituality. Dietrich is particularly interesting in this regard, having exerted, as Hinnebusch observes,

> 'considerable influence on the German mystics, particularly Berthold of Moosburg, Meister Eckhart, and John Tauler.' He demonstrated that a Christian Neoplatonism was reconcilable with monotheism, with the doctrine of creation from nothing, and with the Church's doctrine on grace. At a time when the danger of pantheism and the denial of the supernatural destiny of man were becoming serious, this was a distinct contribution.[28]

Albert's reputation reached much further, of course, some of it spurious, being based on works attributed to him from treatises on alchemy and plant lore to the small mystical treatise

On Cleaving to God (*De Adhaerendo Deo*), which may have come from his circle of disciples.

Master of Mystics

Although Albert occasionally mistook late Neoplatonic writings for Aristotelian commentaries, in the main he was able to balance the excesses of Christian agnosticism associated with Alan of Lille, Amalric of Bene, Gilbert of Poitiers, and other radicals with the positive, critical approach associated with authentic Aristotelian works rediscovered through exposure to Arab commentaries during the twelfth and thirteenth centuries. Around him there developed a philosophical, theological, and mystical school complementary and sometimes antagonistic to that of Paris. It would in the next decades provide Germany, and the world, with some of the greatest preachers and mystics of the Middle Ages, not to mention the controversy and crisis associated with them. Much would pivot on the influence in German Dominican mysticism of the dark knowledge of God inherited from the ancient Church, Albert's lasting legacy.

3. THE DARKNESS OF GOD AND THE NEGATIVE WAY

The young Dominicans who found themselves at the University of Paris also found themselves heir to a mystical tradition stretching back into ancient Israel and as new and exciting as the latest rumours of erroneous doctrine. At the hands of Albert the Great, Thomas of Aquino, and Eckhart of Hochheim, among others, it would develop as a powerful instrument of personal and theological transformation both within the Order of Preachers and throughout the wider reaches of Christendom.

ANCIENT CHRISTIAN WISDOM

In recent years, considerable scholarly attention has been devoted to explaining and analyzing the 'affirmative' and 'negative' dimensions of classical theology, or, to give them their traditional names, *kataphatic* and *apophatic* theology (and by practical extension, spirituality).[1] The terms are ancient, used by Plato, Aristotle, and other Greek authors, for whom *kataphasis* generally meant 'affirmation' and referred logically and grammatically to positive statements, while *apophasis* meant 'denial' or 'negation' and referred to negative statements. The Greek word entered English in the seventeenth century as an ironic rhetorical device by which one denies what one says or does, or 'we really say or advise a thing under a feigned show of passing over, or dissuading it.'[2] But this usage reflects the more subtle use of *apophasis* in Christian mystical theology from Gregory of Nyssa to Nicolas of Cusa.[3]

Credit is usually given to the pseudonymous late fifth-century Christian author known in the Latin West as Dionysius the Areopagite for linking kataphatic and apophatic elements in a theological dialectic in which terms used to designate God are relativized by the logical interplay of necessary opposition.[4] Thus, it is only true to say 'God is good' with the proviso that God is *not* good in the same manner that anything else can be called good. For Dionysius and the tradition that takes its name from him, all positive statements about God must be so qualified.[5] In due time, Albert, Thomas Aquinas, and Meister Eckhart would unstintingly follow this path.

Long before Dionysius, however, the impossibility of adequately describing, much less representing, God was asserted with both the Hebrew tradition and early Christian thought.

THE DARK KNOWLEDGE OF GOD: THE BIBLICAL WITNESS

In the biblical tradition, the repeated emphasis on the impossibility of directly and immediately knowing God, of 'seeing God's face', arises less from the injunction against graven images in Exodus 20:4–5, than vice versa. Certainly in later Jewish and early Christian writings, the theme of 'unknowing', including the sense of God's presence obscured by thick, dark cloud, derives from the earlier Sinai theophanies. But the tradition is paradoxical. Even at this early stage, negative and positive statements are juxtaposed to produce ambiguity and, without doubt, ambivalence.

The darkness enveloping God appears in the opening verses of Genesis: 'The earth was without form and void, and darkness [*choshek*] was upon the face of the deep; and the Spirit of God was moving over the face of the waters' (Gen. 1:2; see also 1:4, 5).

Words such as *choshek* and *'araphel* which convey a sense of thick, enveloping darkness, as well as *'anan* (cloud), are

used to mask the presence of God, as in Exodus 20:21, 'And
the people stood afar off, while Moses drew near to the thick
darkness ['*araphel*] where God was.'[6] God was not always
present in such darkness, however holy it might be: 'Then the
LORD said to Moses, "Stretch out your hand toward heaven
that there may be darkness [*choshek*] over the land of Egypt,
a darkness to be felt." So Moses stretched out his hand toward
heaven, and there was thick darkness in all the land of Egypt
for three days . . .' (Exod. 10:21–2).[7]

The Hiddenness of God

Other devices were used by biblical writers to affirm God's
unknowability, particularly the image of hiddenness used with
still-startling effect by Isaiah: 'Truly, thou art a God who hides
[*cathar*] yourself, O God of Israel, the Saviour' (Isa. 45:15).
Cathar means, variously, 'to be absent', 'to conceal', 'to hide',
or 'to keep something secret'. Isaiah uses it to suggest that
God deliberately hides the divine presence from mortal eyes.
Thus, God's hiddenness is not merely an accident of human
versus divine reality, but *intentional*, meant not least as a lure
to draw humanity forward on its quest for immediacy with
God.[8]

A similar metaphorical affirmation of God's transcendence
is reflected in the complex thematic of seeing God's 'face' or
'countenance', given the lethal consequences or even impossibility of doing so: 'you cannot see my face; for man shall
not see me and live' (Exod. 33:20). But the prohibition is not
absolute. As God tells Moses before the famous 'backward'
theophany, 'there is a place by me where you shall stand upon
the rock; and while my glory passes by I will put you in a cleft
of the rock, and I will cover you with my hand until I have
passed by; then I will take away my hand, and you shall see
my back; but my face shall not be seen' (Exod. 33:21–3).

The Cloud of Unknowing

The most poetic of the biblical metaphors of God's unseen presence, one taken up by early Christian theologians and the author of the fourteenth-century English masterwork, is, as the title of that work affirms, *The Cloud of Unknowing*: 'Cloud [*'anan*] and thick darkness [*'araphel*] are found about him; righteousness and justice are the foundation of his throne' (Ps. 97:2). Often the words for cloud (*'ab, 'anan, 'ananah*, or *shachaq*, Greek, *gnophos*) simply refer to the skies as a measure of God's dominion (see Job 3:5, 36:29, 37:16, 38:18, 37, etc.).

The Cloud of Presence is an entirely different matter. Here, God speaks from the midst of the cloud itself, which becomes an icon of God's abiding presence, later called *shekinah*: 'And as Aaron spoke to the whole congregation of the people of Israel, they looked toward the wilderness, and behold, the glory of the LORD appeared in the cloud [*'anan*]' (Exod. 16:10; see also Num. 12:5, Pss. 99:7, 104:3, etc.). The cloud also serves as God's chariot: 'Behold, the LORD is riding on a swift cloud [*'ab*] and comes to Egypt; and the idols of Egypt will tremble at his presence, and the heart of the Egyptians will melt within them' (Isa. 19: 1; see also Deut. 33:26, Dan. 7:13, etc.).

The Vision of God

Less well-known in the spiritual tradition are those passages that speak of seeing God face-to-face and living to tell of it, as in Genesis 16:13, 'So [Hagar] called the name of the LORD who spoke to her, "Thou art a God of seeing"; for she said, "Have I really seen God and remained alive after seeing him?"' Such experiences are, in fact, foundational: 'So Jacob called the name of the place Peniel, saying, "For I have seen God face to face, and yet my life is preserved"' (Gen. 32:30). Counter-themes exist also in Exodus: 'Thus the LORD used to speak to Moses face to face, as a man speaks to his friend' (Exod. 33:11; see also Num. 6:25–6, 14:13–14, Deut. 5:4–5, 24–7, and

34:10, Judg. 13:21–3, Pss. 4:6, 24:6, 31:16, 67:1, etc., Job 19: 26–7, and Isa. 6:1–5).

Meticulous scriptural exegesis may discern layered traditions with variant understandings of God's accessibility, but the overall biblical witness remains ambiguous. Clearly, however, the tension between seeing–not seeing, knowing–unknowing, like that between God's remoteness and nearness (the transcendence–immanence motif), is present in early documents as well as late ones and scattered throughout the Law, the Prophets, and the Writings. The result is not confusion, however, but paradox, one that will reappear in Christian Scripture and the mystical theology of the young Church.

CHRISTIAN VISION

Early Christian writings are no less ambiguous than the Hebrew Scriptures in regard to the polarities of seeing and knowing the unseen, unknown God. Here, however, qualified knowledge or sight of God is possible through revelation in and through Jesus: 'All things have been delivered to me by my Father; and no one knows the Son except the Father, and no one knows the Father except the Son and anyone to whom the Son chooses to reveal him' (Matt. 11:27). This theme is stated even more emphatically in Luke: ' "All things have been delivered to me by my Father; and no one knows who the Son is except the Father, or who the Father is except the Son and anyone to whom the Son chooses to reveal him." Then turning to the disciples [Jesus] said privately, "Blessed are the eyes which see what you see! For I tell you that many prophets and kings desired to see what you see, and did not see it, and to hear what you hear, and did not hear it" ' (Luke 10:22–4). (For Johannine parallels, see John 1:18, 6:46. But also note 1 John 4:12, 'No man has ever seen God; if we love one another, God abides in us and his love is perfected in us.')

More emphatically, 'Jesus said to [Philip], "Have I been with you so long, and yet you do not know me, Philip? He who has seen me has seen the Father. How can you say, 'Show us the Father'?"' (John 14:9. Similar, Christological confessions are found in John 20:18, 20:25.)

Perhaps the most deliberate affirmation of all is found in 1 John 1:1–3: 'That which was from the beginning, which we have heard, which we have seen with our eyes, which we have looked upon and touched with our hands, concerning the word of life – the life was made manifest, and we saw it, and testify to it, and proclaim to you the eternal life which was with the Father and was made manifest to us. . . .'

Impediments to seeing God remain, however: 'If any one says, "I love God", and hates his brother, he is a liar; for he who does not love his brother whom he has seen, cannot love God whom he has not seen' (1 John 4:20, see also 1 John 3:6 and 3 John 1:11). And the poetic splendour of 1 Timothy remains as a leitmotif of the biblical witness:

> I charge you to keep the commandment unstained and free from reproach until the appearing of our Lord Jesus Christ; and this will be made manifest at the proper time by the blessed and only Sovereign, the King of kings and Lord of lords, who alone has immortality and dwells in unapproachable light, whom no man has ever seen or can see. To him be honor and eternal dominion. Amen. (6:14–16)

THE EMERGENCE OF THE TRADITION

Post-apostolic writers took up the theme of the unknowable God from Hebrew sources, the Greek commentaries of the Intertestamental Period, including the works of Philo in Alexandria, and the teaching of the New Testament. The ambiguity of the previous testimony was perpetuated and refined, often with direct reference to the darkness of Sinai, as in Gregory of Nyssa's highly influential *Life of Moses*.

Long before that, however, Christian writers insisted that despite every effort, we know more what God is not than what

God is: '... God so far surpasses our powers of description
that no one can really give a name to him. Anyone who dares
to say that he can must be hopelessly insane,' wrote Justin
Martyr in Rome in the second century.[9] The anonymous
second-century author of *The Epistle to Diognetus* writes, similarly, 'No one living has ever seen God or known him. God
himself has given us the revelation of himself. But He has only
revealed himself to faith, by which alone are we permitted to
know God' (Ch. 8, 5–6).

With the emergence of an explicit theological tradition in the
third and fourth century, largely in and around the intellectual
centre of Alexandria, where a catechetical school or gym-
nasium was established by the obscure St Pantaenus around
the year 180, the apophatic approach to knowledge of God
and its spiritual correlate was firmly imbedded in Christian
thought and praxis. Pantaenus' successor, Clement of Alexandria, and his own disciple and successor, the great Origen,
acknowledged both the impossibility of directly knowing God
in this life, but also the impetus toward mystical union with
God. For Clement, who adds a metaphysical dimension to the
quest to see God's face, we can attain to God 'not in that which
He is, but in that which He is not.'[10]

Agnosia (unknowing) and *theosis* (deification) thus became
cardinal tenets on which would depend the mystical theology
of the ancient and medieval Church. (It should be recalled that
in its original use, *mystical* simply meant 'hidden', referring
to the known-unknown God of Revelation *and* experience.[11]
But how these tenets were interpreted came to vary widely.

A significant divergence occurred in the fourth century following the rejection of the notion of spiritual affinity between
the human soul and God which had animated the mystical
teaching of Clement and especially Origen and his followers,
including Evagrius of Pontus.[12] For Gregory of Nyssa, Gregory
Nazianzen, Basil, and their followers, God remains wholly
beyond natural human accessibility, cloaked in an eternally
impenetrable cloud of unknowing. What we know of God is
learned only from revelation and held by faith.[13]

Mystical union is possible, but only through love, which draws the soul ever further toward and indeed into the unattainable because infinite Godhead. Common to both schools of thought, however they differ in other respects, is the conviction that while it is impossible to know God directly in this life, we are nevertheless drawn (or driven: *epectasis*) toward ever-increasing closeness to God both in this life and hereafter.

According to Gregory of Nyssa (*c.* 380),

> The vision of God is offered to those who have purified their hearts. Yet, 'no man has seen God at any time.' These are the words of the great Saint John and they are confirmed by Saint Paul's lofty thought, in the words, God is 'he whom no one has seen or can see.' He is that smooth sheer rock, on which the mind can find no secure resting place to get a grip or lift ourselves up. In the view of Moses, he is inaccessible. In spite of every effort, our minds cannot approach him.[14]

For Gregory, in its quest to see God, the mind passes not from darkness to light, but vice versa:

> What does it mean that Moses entered the darkness and then saw God in it? What is now recounted seems somehow to be contradictory to the first theophany, for then the Divine was beheld in light but now he is seen in darkness. Let us not think that this is at variance with the sequence of things we have contemplated spiritually. Scripture teaches by this that religious knowledge comes at first to those who receive it as light. Therefore what is perceived to be contrary to religion is darkness, and the escape from darkness comes about when one participates in light. But as the mind progresses and, through an ever greater and more perfect diligence, comes to apprehend reality, as it approaches more nearly to contemplation, it sees more clearly what of the divine nature is uncontemplated.[15]

Here, Andrew Louth comments, Gregory 'passes beyond the

intellectualism of Origen and the intellectual categories of any Platonic mystical thought and, using the language of the Bible, which speaks of man responding to God with his heart, develops a mysticism that knows God beyond knowledge, that feels the presence of God in the darkness of unknowing.'[16] But, as Louth also reminds us,

> If there is a properly ecstatic element in Gregory's doctrine, it is in the ecstatic nature of love, which continually seeks to draw the soul out of itself to union with God as He is in Himself. Gregory uses both *eros* and *agape* to describe this love, a love which is essentially a desire for union with the beloved. . . . And it is this desire for union which is the principle of the soul's entry into darkness, of the highest stage of the soul's mystical ascent. It is a desire for what is impossible – union with the unknowable God, fed by what is actual – union with God in the soul.[17]

Similarly, for St Gregory of Nazianzen, who employs the image of the darkness of the mind as an overexposure to the divine Light (the 'dazzling darkness' theme),

> If the mind tries to form a faint image of God, considering Him not in Himself but in that which compasses Him, this image eludes it even before it can attempt to seize it, illuminating the superior faculties [of the mind] as a flash of lightning which dazzles the eyes.[18]

In the West, the first great exponent of negative theology was Augustine. 'God is ineffable,' he tells us in the midst of perhaps the richest and most lucid writing about God in all of Christian theology. 'We can more easily say what He is not than what he is.'[19] Again, he says, echoing Athanasius in the East,

> What then, brothers, shall we say of God? For if you have been able to understand what you would say, it is not God. If you have been able to comprehend it, you have comprehended something else than God. If you have been able to comprehend Him as you think, by so thinking you

have deceived yourself. This then is not God, if you have comprehended it; but if this be God, you have not comprehended it. How therefore would you speak of that which you cannot comprehend?[20]

For God 'is more truly thought than expressed; and He exists more truly than He is thought.'[21]

As with Gregory of Nyssa, for Augustine the quest for union with God (at least in this life) is not impelled by nor does it end in objective vision, but by and in love, which draws the soul from the realm of sense, through the 'fields and palaces' of mind and memory, into the vastness of infinite Beauty. 'I ask again, what it is that I love when I love my God? Who is He that is above the topmost point of my soul? By that same soul I shall ascend to Him.'[22] Thus, in the end, union with God is achieved in the re-imaging of the human trinity of memory, understanding, and will by the Trinity of Wisdom, Knowledge, and Love: 'God the Holy Spirit, who proceeds from God, when he is given to man, enkindles in him the love of God and his neighbour, and is that love.'[23]

Later in the fifth century, St Leo the Great (*c.* 450) affirmed for Western thought that 'even if one has progressed far in divine things, one is never nearer the knowledge of truth than when one understands that those things still remain to be discovered. He who believes he has attained the goal, far from finding what he seeks, falls by the wayside.'[24] But the most insistent if yet unsystematic voice of the ancient Church was probably that of the anonymous Greek writer of the late fifth century who called himself Dionysius, after the Athenian convert of St Paul. 'Someone beholding God and understanding what he saw has not actually seen God himself but rather something of his which has being and which is knowable. For he himself solidly transcends mind and being.'[25]

Far more daringly than Augustine, Dionysius weaves the strands of the biblical tradition together with those of the Neo-platonism of his day to produce texts of still-surprising richness and depth.

Just as the senses can neither grasp nor perceive the
things of the mind, just as representation and shape
cannot take in the simple and the shapeless, just as cor-
poral form cannot lay hold of the intangible and
incorporeal, by the same standard of truth beings are
surpassed by the infinity beyond being, intelligences by
that oneness which is beyond intelligence.[26]

A watershed of earlier Greek teaching on the inscrutability
of God, the divine darkness, and the inadequacy of all language
about God, including both positive and negative statements,
the small body of texts ascribed to the Bishop of Athens was
thrown open to the intellectually thirsty scholars of the Middle
Ages by means of a succession of increasingly accurate translations, especially those of John Scottus (Eriugena) and, much
later, John Sarracenus.[27]

THE ENDURING WITNESS

Scottus, an Irish scholar at the French court, made the first
successful Latin translation of the Dionysian corpus about
the year 862. He may have encountered the Greek mystical
tradition in his wanderings, but the following passage from
the Irish missionary, St Columban (c. 543–615) suggests that
the mystical doctrine of the Greek and Latin doctors had penetrated the Church to its farther frontiers much earlier:

Who, I say, shall explore his highest summit to the
measure of this unutterable and inconceivable Being? Who
shall examine the secret depths of God? Who shall dare
to treat of the eternal source of the universe? Who shall
boast of knowing the infinite God, who fills all and sur-
rounds all, who enters into all and passes beyond all, who
occupies all, who escapes all? Whom no man has ever seen
as he is? Therefore let no man venture to seek out the
unsearchable things of God, the nature, mode and cause
of his existence. These are unspeakable, undiscoverable,
unsearchable; only believe in simplicity and yet with

firmness, that God is and shall be even as he has been, since God is immutable.[28]

In the East, shortly afterwards, St John Damascene (c. 700), began his greatest work by similarly denying that any created intellect can understand God: 'God, then, is infinite and incomprehensible, and all that is comprehensible about Him is His infinity and incomprehensibility. All that we can say cataphatically concerning God does not show forth His nature but the things that relate to His nature....'[29]

A century later, Scottus himself insists that

> ... this is the prudent and catholic and salutary profession that is to be predicated of God: that first by the cataphatic, that is by affirmation, we predicate all things of Him, whether by nouns or verbs, though not properly but in a metaphorical sense; then we deny by the apophatic, that is by negation, that He is any of the things which by the cataphatic are predicated of Him, only (this time) not metaphorically but properly – for there is more truth in saying that God is not any of the things that are predicated of Him than in saying that He is.[30]

THE MEDIEVAL RENAISSANCE

During the High Middle Ages, although the paradoxical darkness of divine unknowing became a cornerstone in the mystical epistemology and spiritual doctrine of Albert the Great, Thomas Aquinas and Eckhart, its employment was hardly limited to Dominicans. Nor, of course, was it restricted to Christians, by this time having become a central motif in pagan, Jewish, and Sufi teaching as well.[31]

A significant moment in the Dionysian revolution of the early Middle Ages occurred with the development of the notion that, given the impossibility of secure intellectual comprehension of the Unknowable, Ineffable Deity, only through love could the soul come to 'know' God. This theme was characteristic of the influential views of Thomas Gallus, an Augustinian

canon of St Victor's Abbey in Paris, who became the abbot of
St Andrew's in Vercelli, where he wrote several Dionysian
paraphrases and commentaries. This view was taken up in
turn by Peter of Spain (who later became Pope John XXI), and
Hugh of Balma.[32]

So stated, this doctrine exaggerates the teaching of Dionysius regarding *eros* (love) and *epectasis* (striving) in the quest
for God, but it quickly found favour with those who espoused
the love-mysticism of Augustine and especially St Bernard,
but also favoured the theological scepticism of Alan of Lille
and other radicals. It would, for example, appear in a moderate
form in *The Cloud of Unknowing* toward the end of the fourteenth century.

Matters came to a head in 1241, when the Bishop of Paris
engineered the condemnation of many of the more extreme
versions of theological and mystical agnosticism. But the controversies hardly ended with this ecclesiastical intervention.
The theological faculty of the University of Paris itself was
now fast becoming the final arbiter in matters of doctrinal
orthodoxy, and the masters were divided on these and many
related issues.

Towards the end of the final chapter of *The Soul's Journey
into God*, St Bonaventure cautiously cites Dionysius to bring
his masterpiece to a fitting conclusion:

> ... little importance should be given to words and to
> writing, but all to the gift of God, that is, the Holy Spirit;
> little or no importance should be given to creation, but all
> to the creative essence, the Father, Son and Holy Spirit,
> saying with Dionysius to God the Trinity: 'Trinity, superes-
> sential, superdivine and supereminent overseer of the
> divine wisdom of Christians, direct us into the super-
> unknown, superluminous and most sublime summit of
> mystical communication. There new, absolute and
> unchangeable mysteries of theology are hidden in the
> superluminous darkness of a silence teaching secretly in
> the utmost obscurity which is supermanifest – a darkness

which is super-resplendent and in which everything shines forth and which fills to overflowing invisible intellects with the splendors of invisible goods that surpass all good' [Dionysius, *De mystica theologia*, 1, 1]. This is said to God. But to the friend to whom these words were written, let us say with Dionysius: 'But you, my friend, . . . concerning mystical visions, with your journey more firmly determined, leave behind your senses and intellectual activities, sensible and invisible things, all nonbeing and being; and in this state of unknowing be restored, insofar as is possible, to unity with him who is above all essence and knowledge. For transcending yourself and all things, by the immeasurable and absolute ecstasy of a pure mind, leaving behind all things and freed from all things, you will ascend to the superessential ray of the divine darkness.'[33]

In the following centuries, the organic, if not quite systematic, integrity of the Dionysian theological dialectic, which balanced positive and negative affirmations of God, all of which were deemed inadequate and, at best, approximative, was gradually dismantled. Negative theology was increasingly sundered from its positive counterpart. Restoring the symbolic synthesis, simultaneously cosmic and liturgical, became the task and to a great extent the accomplishment of Albert the Great and Thomas Aquinas. But even their genius was unable to prevent the *via negativa* from assuming a disproportionate influence in the later Middle Ages.

Eventually, under the influence of theologians such as Jean Gerson, who became chancellor of the University of Paris in 1395, the rift between mind and heart was widened, and with it, that between theology and spirituality. The triumph of the *devotio moderna* in the fifteenth century, particularly as proposed in *The Imitation of Christ*, signals the emergence of an approach to God rich in feeling, especially of a penitential tone, but lacking the intellectual vigour and mystical aspirations of the High Middle Ages.

CONCLUSION: A PERENNIAL PERSPECTIVE

A certain characteristic enthusiasm on the part of great Dominican writers and mystics such as Albert, Thomas, and Eckhart, among others, for the paradoxical and problematic approach to God through knowing-unknowing is thus not only preceded (and followed) by that of a cloud of other witnesses; it would be far more surprising were it missing from their teaching. But the fact that these outstanding Dominican scholars and mystics, and the tradition that looks back to them from *The Cloud of Unknowing* to John of the Cross, found in this ancient doctrine the cornerstone of their theology and spirituality warrants closer examination.

4. KNOWING THE UNKNOWABLE GOD: THE THREEFOLD PATH OF THOMAS AQUINAS

With the exception of St Augustine, no single individual has had the pronounced influence on Christian theology as the quiet Italian friar once dubbed 'the Dumb Ox' by his fellow students and known to the world as Thomas Aquinas. Thomas of Aquino is remembered less as a spiritual writer than a philosopher and theologian. Yet, as Fr Jean-Pierre Torrel has shown, following the example of the epoch-making study of Fr M.-D. Chenu, Thomas' scholarly work was inseparable from and indeed rooted in his personal spirituality, itself grounded in his Dominican identity. Further, his teaching inevitably leads to spiritual application.[1] Torrell affirms

> not only that the saint is inseparable from the philosopher or the theologian, but that these three figures are also accompanied by a 'spiritual master.' Growing reflection on the faith was a path to sanctity for Thomas and it shows in his works. There is in this an entire dimension of his teaching that is certainly familiar to those who closely study it over time, but that generally escapes those who have only a sketchy acquaintance with Thomas. This leads to a considerable loss and it suffices to point it out to experience the benefit of a different reading of Thomas.[2]

Thus, he proposes to show 'how the theology overflows into the spiritual life or, if one wishes, into mysticism.'[3] Over a generation ago, Fr Raymond Martin observed, similarly, 'There is no mystical doctrine more human nor more divine than the spiritual doctrine elaborated by the Angel of the Schools. . . . Saint Thomas is the Prince of Mystical Theology.'[4]

A SCHOLAR'S LIFE

Born in the winter of 1225–6, Thomas was the eleventh child and youngest son of Lord Landulf and Lady Theodora of Aquino, a noble German-Italian family whose principal residence was at Roccasecca, near Naples. At the age of five, his parents sent him for schooling to the Benedictines at nearby Monte Cassino, expecting that he would someday become abbot.

Around 1239, when Thomas was thirteen, Monte Cassino was seized by the Emperor, Frederick II, and the monks expelled. Thomas returned home, but at the recommendation of his teachers at the abbey, he was sent for further study to the University of Naples. There, he was deeply impressed by the philosophy of Aristotle, recently introduced by one of his teachers, Peter of Ireland. Thomas also met the Dominicans and was befriended by one of them, John of San Giuliano. Strongly attracted by the innovative blend of scholarship with evangelical poverty, preaching, and a simple gospel style of life, Thomas was advised by his friend to seek admission to the Order.

Thomas' family was appalled when Thomas was clothed in the Dominican habit. Hoping to bring him to his senses, his brothers kidnapped him and for over fifteen months attempted in various ways to 'deprogram' him. Ox-like, the teenager resisted every inducement to abandon his new commitment, and was finally freed from confinement through the intervention of his mother.

Sent to the Dominican house of studies at the University of Paris, Thomas completed his novitiate in 1245. He soon fell under the influence of one of the most powerful minds of the age – Albert of Lauingen, who according to legend quickly perceived the original brilliance of the big 'dumb ox' scorned by the other students. In 1248 the great German philosopher, theologian, and scientist chose Thomas to accompany him to Cologne to establish a new *studium generale*, which soon became the nub of another university. There the young Dominican finished his initial studies, was ordained a priest in 1250, and was soon sent back to teach in Paris and become a master in sacred theology – the highest academic honour of the time.

Almost immediately, he found himself embroiled in disputes with the other masters, much of it centring on the use of Aristotle by Albert, Thomas, and other radicals. Thomas was suspect also because of his affiliation with the Dominicans, who along with the Franciscans and other mendicants, were resented and despised by the traditional faculty and many bishops.

A brilliant debater, Thomas bested some of the keenest minds in the university in formal disputation, including the future Bishop of Paris, Stephen Tempier, and the future Archbishop of Canterbury, John Pecham, both of whom took pains to assure that his teaching was condemned at the Universities of Paris and Oxford after Thomas' premature death in 1274. But if immersed in controversy during most of his academic career, Thomas also had important friends and allies, not least of whom were King Louis IX of France and Pope Urban IV.

It was at Paris in 1259 that Thomas began work on his first masterpiece, the *Summa Contra Gentiles*, intended as a manual for missionaries working among non-Christians. He moved to Naples the same year to teach at the university, then, from 1261 to 1265 taught at Orvieto, the papal residence of Urban IV, where he composed at the pope's request the liturgy for the Feast of Corpus Christi, the most elegantly poetic and deeply religious of all Thomas' works.

In Rome by 1264, now 38 years of age, Thomas began work on his great *Summa Theologiae*, which he envisioned as an introduction for beginning students. It would occupy him until his death ten years later. During that decade, he also taught at Viterbo and, from 1269 to 1272, was back in Paris for a second tenure as Regent Master during a particularly critical period. The secular masters of the university had mounted another serious offensive against the Dominicans and Franciscans, just as the teachings of Aristotle had come under renewed fire.

Thomas was deeply involved in both controversies, but by the end of 1272 had returned to Naples to teach. There, on 6 December 1273, he suffered what appears to have been a stroke which left him partially impaired in speech and unable to write. Summoned by the pope to the Ecumenical Council at Lyons, at which, it was hoped, Eastern and Western Christendom would be reunited, Thomas left for France early the following year. Apparently riding on a mule because of his illness, he struck his head against an overhanging branch unnoticed by his companions, who were on foot. At first, he seemed unharmed, but gradually it became evident that he had sustained a head injury, probably a subdural hematoma.

Taken to the nearby home of his sister, Francesca, his condition worsened. Realizing that death was near, Thomas asked to be taken to a religious house. At the Cistercian abbey of Fossanuova, he died on 7 March in the company of his fellow friars, both Franciscan and Dominican, as well as the monks and several relatives.

Within three years, Thomas' old opponent, Bishop Stephen Tempier, and Edward Kilwardby, the Dominican Archbishop of Canterbury, succeeded in having over one hundred propositions from his works condemned as heretical because of their Aristotelian flavour. At Oxford, the 1277 condemnation was repeated in 1284 by Kilwardby's successor, John Pecham.

Thomas' supporters resisted strenuously. In 1309, the Dominican Order declared Thomas' teaching to be the official doctrine of the Order. By 1315, complete copies of his writings were ordered to be made available in all houses of study and major priories. Two years later, materials were gathered to support his canonization, and on 14 July 1323, Pope John XXII enrolled Thomas among the saints. In 1325, the Bishop of Paris revoked the condemnation of 1277. Thomas was never formally 'rehabilitated' at Oxford. In 1567, however, he was declared a Doctor of the Church. And in 1880, Pope Leo XIII recognized Thomas as the patron of all Catholic universities.

THE FRUITS OF CONTEMPLATION

Like his teacher, Albert the Great, Thomas filled shelves with his writings on Scripture, theology, and philosophy. Over one hundred works ascribed to Thomas are considered to be authentic, many of them consisting of several volumes. Although justly famed for his huge handbooks, the *Summa Contra Gentiles* and the unfinished *Summa Theologiae*, Thomas would have understood himself primarily as a Scripture scholar.[5] He composed no works that might be identified by contemporary standards as spirituality. Like his predecessors in the Greek and Latin Churches, he would not have considered it necessary, as a profound spirituality informs all his writings. His commentaries on the Gospels, especially the Gospel of John, include his finest contributions, and his eucharistic hymns, especially the *Pange Lingua* and *Lauda Sion*, are beloved throughout the world.

Surprisingly, despite its importance for spiritual theology, Thomas' Commentary on *The Divine Names* of Dionysius has not been translated into English. Yet his use of that book and the other writings of Dionysius indicate that he not only knew the teaching thoroughly, but employed it despite the Neoplatonic cast of its outlook.

THOMAS' SPIRITUALITY

His personal holiness of life was well known to Thomas' confrères and even among the wider public, so much so that, as with St Dominic, there was controversy between the friars and the monks where the two saints lay dying over the possession of their bodies because of the mania for relics that existed at the time.

Writing just over a generation after his death, one of the Order's more reliable historians, Bernard Gui (1279–1331) stated,

In St Thomas the habit of prayer was extraordinarily

developed. He seemed to be able to raise his mind to God
as if the body's burden did not exist for him. At night,
when our nature demands repose, he would rise after a
short sleep and pray, lying prostrate on the ground. It was
in those nights of prayer that he would learn what he
would write or dictate in the daytime.[6]

Gui cites eyewitness testimony regarding Thomas' profound
mystical states, when he was deeply entranced, his face bathed
in tears, and also his deep, personal devotion to the Eucharist.[7]
In an era in which it was still unusual, Thomas said mass
daily and normally attended a second mass, serving as an
acolyte.

Citing the *Processus canonizationis* from Naples, and the
Life by Gui, Hinnebusch observes that:

Thomas himself was a contemplative who possessed the
eminent knowledge and love that he wrote about. These
had come to him from above rather than from his own
study and labor. Before every major occupation, whether
debating, teaching, writing, or dictating, he had recourse
to prayer. His ardent love for God revealed itself in his
fervent prayer before the Crucifix, in his intense love for
the Sacrament of the Altar. His mystical intuition of divine
things and his burning desire for union with God carried
him at times into ecstasy. His mystical experiences
reached such intensity toward the end of his life that all
he had written seemed to him 'so much straw.' Forced to
lay down his pen, he confessed that he could write no
more.[8]

This is, of course, a reference to what Weisheipl and others
consider a cerebral accident, which, however, does not preclude
the possibility of a mystical experience before, during, or afterwards. Earlier, that is before 6 December, according to a
witness, Bro. Dominic of Ceserta, the sacristan of the priory
chapel,

Praying before the Crucifix early in December, 1273,

[Thomas] had a vision which heralded his death three months later. Rapt beyond his senses and raised toward the Cross, he heard the Crucified address him: 'You have written well of me, Thomas. What do you desire as a reward for your labors?' The answer that fell from his lips revealed that his lifetime search for wisdom in all its forms was spurred on by his unending quest for the Eternal Wisdom: 'Nothing but Thyself, O Lord.'[9]

KNOWING AND UNKNOWING GOD

Thomas builds his teaching on the spiritual life on his understanding of the human person and his understanding of God and our relationship to God. In the *Summa Theologiae*, Thomas begins with God, logically enough, for the framework of his most mature and influential work is the Apostles' Creed. But in most respects it is easier to begin with the human world, Thomas' 'theological anthropology', which occupies the bulk of the *Summa*.

The Holiness of Wholeness

First of all, Thomas sees human persons as a spiritual unity of mind and body, although once actually existing, the mind or soul can operate and continue in existence independently of its material embodiment, if imperfectly. Thomas is a moderate dualist in this respect, refusing to reduce mental reality or experience to physical functions or to regard the body as a dispensable adjunct of the mind. After death, the soul is thus incompletely human and requires physical incorporation for its ultimate beatitude, which Thomas firmly acknowledges as the intent of the Christian belief in the resurrection of the body.

Human powers and activities are divided for him into those that are properly spiritual (intelligence and will, principally expressed as knowledge and love), fundamentally physical (sensation and other bodily functions and behaviour), and those which are mixed (imagination and memory). Existentially, all our activities are holistic expressions of the unity of the human person, a view directly opposite that of Cartesian dualism or even psycho-physical parallelism. For Thomas, just as the physical and psychological dimensions of the person are organized and integrated according to their form and function, so the spiritual life has its intrinsic harmony, one which does not duplicate or mirror the psycho-physical, but completes or 'perfects' it. The moral and intellectual powers are internally developed by habits derived from experience and guided by conscience and the external codes of custom and law.

Spiritually, the human organism is further enhanced by divine grace operating through the theological virtues (habits of right action) of faith, hope, and charity. The 'gifts of the Holy Spirit', the 'beatitudes', and 'the fruits of the Holy Spirit', which Thomas adopts from Scripture and traditional Christian spiritual theology, complete the operational, dynamic 'pneumatology' that structures the spiritual life, culminating in ever-closer intimacy with God in this life and ultimate beatitude hereafter.

There is nothing daringly original in Thomas' integrative vision of the full range of human potential and operation. But certain features of his encompassing and systematic doctrine are worth noting. First, unlike many of his contemporaries, Thomas maintains a balanced and healthy respect for the body in his spiritual teaching, including areas of contemporary interest such as diet and nutrition, exercise, hygiene, and sexuality. Second, in contrast to the growing tendency of his time to exalt the will over intelligence, Thomas insists on the primacy of the mind in regard to both earthly experience and eternal beatitude. Third, however, love in both its ordinary and theological senses enjoys enormous importance in Thomas' scheme of things. He insists, much like his Franciscan counterparts Bonaventure and Duns Scotus, that in our lives as pilgrims and wayfarers, love unites us more closely to God than does knowledge, which remains incapable of attaining to the direct (much less comprehensive) vision of God.[10] Here,

Thomas not only builds upon the apophatic element in Christian theology and spirituality in his teaching, but like Bonaventure, the *Cloud* author, and Meister Eckhart, he places divine and human friendship at the very centre of the spiritual life.

Despite his consistent emphasis on the superiority of the intellect, Thomas was not a rationalist in the later, Enlightenment sense of the term. He considered the intellect to be superior to the will, not 'better', but ontologically 'higher', being more akin to the divine nature itself. For Thomas, however, it is no less true to say that 'God is love' than 'God is truth' and he maintains the primacy of charity in approaching union with God in this life and the next.

The Mystery of God

The second element supporting Thomas' spiritual doctrine is his fundamental theology, that is, his teaching about the divine nature and our relationship to God, especially how we can know and meaningfully talk about God. Here, Thomas draws most conspicuously on the themes of his great Greek and Latin predecessors, particularly Dionysius.[11]

For Thomas, as for most medieval theologians, the terms of the discussion about knowing and naming God were framed by Augustine's dictum, 'God is more truly thought than expressed; and He exists more truly than he is thought.'[12] Thomas' negative theological pathway thus has three distinct though interlaced levels or tiers: first, the linguistic or expressive; second, the psychological and epistemological; and, third, the ontological and theological. Briefly, words invariably fall short of our mental apprehension of the divine Reality which evades all conceptualization.

But for Thomas, when it comes to knowing God the inadequacy of speech and thought is not absolute. However inadequate our names for God, who remains nameless in that no single name properly expresses the divine essence, we do point in the right direction with the multitude of names based on our perceptions of divine qualities inherent in creation as well as revealed in Scripture.

Although arduous, thinking our way through to some understanding of what we mean by 'God', that is, naming God accurately and positively, is not for Thomas merely an intellectual exercise, an academic pursuit devoid of moral and mystical implications. As Jacques Maritain says with regard to Thomas' famous 'Five Ways' of pointing to divine Reality,

> ... to demonstrate the existence of God is not to subject Him to our grasp, nor to define or lay hold on Him, nor to manipulate anything other than ideas which are inadequate to such an object, nor to judge anything except our rightful and radical dependence. The process by which reason demonstrates that God exists, places reason itself in an *attitude of natural adoration and intellectual admiration.*[13]

For Thomas, as for Bonaventure, Eckhart, and the medieval tradition from Anselm to Ockham, the normal path from theological speculation to prayer remains not only continuous, but reciprocal. But for Thomas, as we shall see, even short of contemplative insight, we do know *something* about God, not despite the limitations imposed by negative theology, but because of them.

God's Transcendence

In his various treatments of knowing and not-knowing God, Thomas typically begins by adverting to divine transcendence, the utter difference between God and everything else. For Thomas, God is not the supreme being, because God is not 'a' being at all. God is, however, supremely *Being*, the font of all existence, the ultimate reason why anything at all exists. But there is no proportion, therefore, between God's existence and that of anything else. The divine Reality evades all categories of being as well as thought just as it grounds and pervades them. As a result, 'God is said to have no name, or to be beyond naming, because his essence is beyond what we understand of him and the meaning of the names we use.'[14]

Not-Knowing God

Negative theology, our acknowledgement that God is not merely 'more' but always ineffably beyond the categories of human thought, safeguards both the dignity of human intelligence and the theological enterprise itself, which would otherwise veer dangerously close to presumption if not idolatry. As Thomas says, 'It is because human intelligence is not equal to the divine essence that this same divine essence surpasses our intelligence and is unknown to us: wherefore one reaches the highest point of knowledge about God when one knows that he does not know God, inasmuch as one knows that that which is God transcends whatsoever one conceives of him.'[15]

'Unknowing' is thus a way of knowing the unknowable God. For in Thomas' view, negative knowledge produces positive effects:

> ... the human mind advances in three ways in knowing God, though it does not reach a knowledge of what he is (*quid est*), but only that he is (*an est*). First, by knowing more perfectly his power in producing things. Second, by knowing him as the cause of more lofty effects which, because they bear some resemblance to him, give more praise to his greatness. Third, by an ever-growing knowledge of him as distant from everything that appears in his effects. Thus Dionysius says that we know God as the cause of all things, by transcendence and by negation.[16]

God-Talk

Against Rabbi Moses Maimonides and those Christian thinkers such as Alan de Lille who held that none of our words for God actually signify the Divine Reality but are mere pointers to what remains absolutely unknowable, Thomas thus asserts that certain terms, based on our intimations of God in creation, as well as those divinely revealed in Scripture, really, if inadequately, refer to God. These include being, unity, and goodness. But although such positive predicates indicate something about God, Thomas reminds us that it is truer to say that they tell us what God is not rather than what God is.[17]

For Thomas, as for Dionysius seven hundred years earlier, negative theology is founded upon and necessarily corrects positive theology. It gives us some knowledge of God. At best, however, our theological precisions are fuzzy:

> ... the idea of negation is always based on an affirmation: as evinced by the fact that every negative proposition is proved by an affirmative: wherefore unless the human mind knew something positively about God, it would be unable to deny anything about him. And it would know nothing if nothing that it affirmed about God were positively verified about him. Hence following Dionysius (*The Divine Names*, 13) we must hold that these terms signify the divine essence, *albeit defectively and imperfectly*. ...
>
> Accordingly we conclude that each of these terms signifies the divine essence, *not comprehensively but imperfectly*. ... This solution of the question is confirmed by the words of Dionysius (*The Divine Names*, 1): 'Since all things are comprised in the Godhead simply and without limit, it is fitting that he should be praised and named on account of them all: simply, because the perfections which are in creatures by reason of various forms are ascribed to God in reference to his simple essence; and without limit, because no perfection found in creatures is equal to the divine essence, so as to enable the mind under the head of that perfection to define God as he is in himself.'[18]

For Thomas, there is no untruth, therefore, in the affirmation that 'The heavens are telling the glory of God; and the firmament proclaims his handiwork' (Ps. 19:1; cf. Ps. 97:6), or that in daily experiences of love and compassion, we see the face of the Transcendent. But such knowledge is always limited and incomplete.

THOMAS' THREE WAYS OF KNOWING AND UNKNOWING GOD

Thomas thus follows (and develops) the insights of the ancient Christian tradition regarding the three ways of understanding and speaking about the transcendent God. The first is the *via positiva*, or affirmative way, which allows us to make definite but limited statements about God, such as the fact that God exists, God is good, etc. Second is the *via negativa* or *remotionis*, by which, so far as their limitations are concerned, such notions are negated or denied. As we encounter being, goodness, and wisdom in the things about us, they cannot belong to God in exactly the same sense, but they do mirror their Creator. The third way, the *via eminentiae* or way of transcendence, goes beyond both affirmation and denial, proceeding on the assurance that such attributes, reflected analogously in our experience of creation, must exist in God in a much higher, ultimately imponderable manner.[19]

We therefore come closest to accurately expressing this conception of the Transcendent God when we say not merely that God loves, but that 'God is Love' (1 John 4:8, 16), or that God is Goodness or Beauty themselves, or, with the philosophers, God does not merely exist, God is Being itself. But, Thomas maintains, characteristically,

> The human mind receives its greatest help in this advance of knowledge when its natural light is strengthened by a new illumination, like the light of faith and the gifts of wisdom and understanding, through which the mind is said to be raised above itself in contemplation, inasmuch as it knows that God is above everything it naturally comprehends.[20]

Ultimately, however, the face of God remains beyond mortal vision, and what little we know about God, whether intuitively or reflectively, is sighted through a glass, darkly, as Paul insists. We encounter God more truly in prayer, sacrament, and service.

THOMAS' SPIRITUAL DOCTRINE

Although there is no extensive discussion of the spiritual life in Thomas' writings other than what pertains to all Christians, he devoted a section of the *Summa Theologiae* to issues of his time concerning the spirituality of the mendicant orders, which were under almost constant attack by the diocesan clergy at the University of Paris. Despite its defensive and polemical aspects, this section contains some of Thomas' most probing insights into Christian spirituality in general.[21]

He first considers the extraordinary aspects of the spiritual life that grabbed people's attention then and still do: prophecy, rapture, miracles, the gift of tongues, and the grace of the word, specifically preaching (about which, see below). Surprisingly, Thomas considers such irruptions of grace into human affairs to be within the normal range of Christian experience, if admittedly rare. He thus refuses to countenance a two-track approach to God, one for the common herd, the other for a spiritual elite.

Thomas next deals with various problems arising from the tension between action and contemplation. Finally, he develops his doctrine on the various states of life, discussing the nature of spiritual development, particularly in the episcopal and religious states. Thomas' main concern is to show that the characteristic activities of the mendicant orders, teaching, preaching, the abandonment of manual labour for study, and reliance on alms, are compatible with religious life as traditionally understood. But his defence also contains teaching relevant to all Christians, especially the pre-eminence of the 'mixed' or apostolic life which, he argues, excels both the purely contemplative and active forms of life, as Diego de Acabes and Dominic had come to realize seventy years before.

For these are not only characteristic themes in Thomas'

writing, they represent an index of his contribution to Dominican spirituality as well as the legacy he received from it.

A LASTING INHERITANCE

Thomas' spiritual doctrine, which is to say, the spirituality of his doctrine, remained an enduring legacy during the coming centuries. Within the Order of Preachers, his influence was profound on both those who followed him closely and freer spirits. Among Dominican spiritual writers and preachers who looked to Thomas are found the names of Meister Eckhart, John and Gerard Sterngassen, Nicholas of Strassburg, John Tauler, Henry Suso, and John of St Thomas (Jean Poinsot), to mention only some of the most prominent. Beyond the immediate confines of the Order, Thomas is cited by the *Cloud* author, the Carmelite mystics of the sixteenth and seventeenth centuries, and many of the great Jesuit authors.

THOMAS THE DOMINICAN

In assessing the place of distinctive Dominican themes in Thomas' teaching, not only does he incorporate them into his spiritual doctrine, they are the pillars on which it stands. After all, his great Summas were primarily written for members of the Order, especially the younger brethren.

The Priority of Preaching

In the *Summa Theologiae*, throughout his treatment of contemplation and the life of religious perfection, Thomas stresses the importance of the preaching ministry, seeing in it the grounds for asserting the superiority of mixed orders, that is those which combine action and contemplation, over those which are only contemplative (or, for that matter, merely active). Central to his argument are the interconnected elements of prayer, common life, and the study of Scripture.

First of all, as Hinnebusch tells us,

In his *Summa Theologiae*, St Thomas discusses the special
graces of which St Paul speaks in his first Epistle to the
Corinthians, such as the grace of working miracles or
prophesying (*Summa theol.*, II–II, q. 177). Among these
Paul classes the grace of the word (*gratia sermonis et
sapientiae, et scientiae*) (I Cor. 12:8). This is a preeminent
grace given sometimes to the preacher, teacher, or writer,
not for his own spiritual benefit but so that he may more
effectively instruct those who listen to him, that he may
move them to hear the word of God eagerly and with joy
and that he may induce them to love his doctrine and
carry it out. Women also, Thomas writes, even though
they do not teach as bishops and priests do, may receive
this grace when they teach the word of God....[22]

Contemplation and Poverty of Spirit

Thomas addresses several questions in the *Summa Theologiae*
to the notion of contemplation, at once both the heart of Dominican spirituality and a major bone of contention with the
secular clergy at the University of Paris.[23]

... the work of the active life is twofold. One proceeds
from the fullness of contemplation, such as teaching and
preaching.... And this work is more excellent than simple
contemplation. For even as it is better to enlighten than
merely to shine, so is it better to give to others what has
been contemplated than merely to contemplate. The other
work of the active life consists entirely in outward occupation, for instance almsgiving, receiving guests, and the
like, which are less excellent than the works of contemplation, except in cases of necessity, as stated above (Q182,
A1). Accordingly the highest place in religious orders is
held by those which are directed to teaching and
preaching, which, moreover, are nearest to the episcopal
perfection, even as in other things 'the end of that which
is first is in conjunction with the beginning of that which is

second,' as Dionysius states (*The Divine Names*, 8). The second place belongs to those which are directed to contemplation, and the third to those which are occupied with external actions.

So much is clear, and while grating to the seculars, not too surprising coming from a member of a mixed order. But Thomas integrates preaching and contemplation with a prudent but evangelical poverty in a still-surprising move. He asks (II–II, Q. 188, A. 7), 'Whether religious perfection is diminished by possessing something in common?' And he answers,

> Now it is manifest that a religious order established for the purpose of contemplating and of giving to others the fruits of one's contemplation by teaching and preaching, requires greater care of spiritual things than one that is established for contemplation only. Wherefore it becomes a religious order of this kind to embrace a poverty that burdens one with the least amount of care ... this being accomplished by their laying up the necessaries of life procured at a fitting time. This, our Lord, the Founder of poverty, taught by His example. For He had a purse which He entrusted to Judas, and in which were kept the things that were offered to Him, as related in John 12:6.

The Primacy of Truth and the Bond of Love

Thomas not only wrote three large volumes on Truth, *De Veritate*, the notion of truth pervades each of his works. It is largely because of his infatuation with Divine Truth, not merely semantic or philosophical accuracy, that it has become the most well-known motto of the Order. And, as Josef Pieper reminds us, Truth, for Thomas, refers to all-encompassing Reality.

Finally, with regard to the role of charity in the contemplative ministry, a point that Eckhart will later cite (and, in fact, elaborate) from Thomas' teaching, Aquinas himself was abundantly clear:

Sometimes a person is called away from the contemplative life to the works of the active life on account of some necessity of the present life, yet not so as to be compelled to forsake contemplation altogether. . . . [and here he cites Augustine]: 'if it be imposed on us, we must bear it because charity demands it of us . . .' [*de Civ. Dei*, xix, 19]. Hence it is clear that when a person is called from the contemplative to the active life, this is done not by way of subtraction, but of addition.[24]

CONCLUSION

In the end, for Thomas (and, he would argue, for everyone) God is not so much an object to be thought or even thought about, much less discussed endlessly, as a Presence to be sought. The art of such seeking is contemplative action, and its end is mystical union, both in this life and hereafter.

Thomas and his later contemporary, Meister Eckhart, also a disciple of Albert the Great, often seem to represent opposite sides of Albert's philosophical personality, the Aristotelian and the Neoplatonic. In some regards, they could hardly be further apart in their approach.[25] In other respects, their doctrine is remarkably alike. But when describing the contemplative dimension of the Christian life, and its unity of charity, they could hardly be closer together, as we shall next see.

5. MEISTER ECKHART'S WAYLESS WAY AND THE NOTHINGNESS OF GOD

Apophatic mysticism encompasses a wide range of styles and positions from the conservative ruminations of Athanasius, Augustine, and Dionysius to the lyrical and imaginative flights of the author of *The Cloud of Unknowing*. Even further toward the edge are Meister Eckhart's rhetorical fireworks. He seems to have delighted in shocking his listeners into attention to the divine presence within and in the world outside by outrageous comparisons, puns, and comic examples. But like Till Eulenspiegel, by adopting the role of trickster Eckhart irritated the official guardians of pious sobriety and cautious expression, first the uncompromising Archbishop of Cologne, Heinrich von Virneburg, who proved to be his nemesis, and then the watchdogs of orthodoxy attached to the papal court at Avignon, who, like the English Franciscan philosopher, William of Ockham, condemned Eckhart's playful but profound assaults on conventional God-talk as mad and dangerous.

In this respect, Eckhart stands alongside Socrates, Jesus, Mansur al-Hallaj, and a multitude of Zen masters and Hasidic rabbis whose keen and deadly word-play stimulated the imagination and fed the souls of their followers, but stung the sensibilities of religious and civil authorities, sometimes to the point of lethal reprisal.[1] Close to the heart of Eckhart's message lay the chief tenets of the ancient Christian tradition of negative theology, or, in his terms, the darkness or nothingness of God, and the necessity of radical detachment.

A PREACHER'S LIFE

Eckhart of Hochheim was born about 1260 in a Thuringian village in north-eastern Germany near the town of Erfurt. Nothing is known of his family, birth, or childhood. At about the age of fifteen, he entered the Dominican novitiate at Erfurt.

As a student friar, Eckhart was sent to Cologne in 1280 for his initial studies. There he seems to have met the aged Albert the Great. 'Bishop Albrecht' died in the autumn of that year, but Eckhart was surely taught by some of his disciples. He became an ardent if selective follower of Thomas Aquinas, but he absorbed even more readily the ancient mystical tradition of Christian Neoplatonism favoured by several of Albert's students, particularly Dietrich of Freiberg.[2]

After finishing his studies at Cologne, Eckhart was ordained to the priesthood, probably in 1293. That year he was sent to Paris as a lecturer and to begin studies for the coveted title of Master. Even so, he was soon elected to a number of important positions in the Dominican Order. In 1294, he became Prior of Erfurt. About the same time, he was also appointed Vicar of Thuringia. Four years later, after the terms of office expired, Eckhart was finally able to finish his studies. In 1302, nine years after his departure for Paris, he was granted the title of *Magister in theologia*, the highest academic honour of the age.

Eckhart was now forty-three. After a year as Regent Master for Externs at St Jacques, the Dominican house of studies in Paris, he was elected first provincial of the new Province of Saxony, which included Erfurt. He was also charged with the spiritual guidance of the Dominican nuns of the region.

For some time, large numbers of Beguines had been flocking to Dominican convents. What attracted them and large numbers of other devout, well-educated women to the Dominicans in the late thirteenth and early fourteenth centuries was, it appears, the emphasis placed on study in the order together with the mystical character of its spirituality. The encounter between dynamic preachers and these God-centred women produced one of the most spectacular upsurges of mystical spirituality in the history of Europe.

Both Dominican and Franciscan friars had also been charged with the spiritual direction of other Beguine houses which were not formally related to either order. Whole convents of other religious orders had also changed their affiliation to the Dominicans, and several new foundations were made. The friars were faced with an explosion of vocations and extensive responsibilities, and Eckhart was in the centre of it all.

In 1307, the Chapter of Strassburg appointed Eckhart Vicar of Bohemia and commissioned him to reform the houses there. Between 1309 and 1310, he also founded three new communities. He was then elected provincial of the Teutonian province. But this election was overturned by the General Chapter which met at Naples the following spring. The Meister was needed again in Paris. There, in addition to teaching, Eckhart began his great *Opus Tripartitum* ('The Three-Part Work') which he intended to be his crowning academic achievement.

But Eckhart was not destined to finish his masterwork. In 1313 he was recalled to Germany, where he became professor of theology, spiritual director, and preacher in the exciting city of Strassburg. In 1314, he may have been elected prior there, but soon afterwards was named vicar by the Master of the Order, who once more placed Eckhart in charge of the Dominican nuns of the southern Rhineland.

After several years of preaching, teaching, and spiritual direction in Strassburg and its environs, Eckhart was recalled to Cologne in 1322 to serve as regent master of the *studium generale*. But three years later, at the age of sixty-six, he was summoned before the inquisition of the Archbishop of Cologne, the formidable Henry of Virneburg, under the accusation of preaching heresy.

For over a year, Eckhart vigorously defended himself, claiming that the charges were lodged out of jealousy and pursued out of ignorance. But the verdict went against him. Outraged, and with the support of his superior and fellow friars, he appealed to the pope. And thus at the age of sixty-seven or sixty-eight, Eckhart and several friends began the five hundred mile trek to the papal court at Avignon to plead his case.

The process dragged on for more than a year. Before a judgement was reached, the old friar died, some historians believe on the feast of St Thomas Aquinas, 28 January 1328, having first retracted anything that could be proved heretical in his teachings. But he also continued to deny that either his intention or actual words were in fact contrary to the faith.

At the Archbishop's insistence, Pope John XXII issued a bull of condemnation in March, 1329, and ordered it to be promulgated in the area of Cologne. Unfortunately, its effect was far more widespread. Not only had Eckhart been the most famous preacher of his day, but the first member of the Dominican Order to be tried for heresy. His teachings were suppressed, his memory tainted. Many of his writings were subsequently lost or destroyed. Not even his grave site has been discovered.

But condemnation could not dispel the memory of Eckhart's teaching, which was honoured by the Dominican friars and nuns throughout the Rhineland. Nearly six hundred excerpts from Eckhart's commentary on John's Gospel copied by the friars at Cologne were discovered as late as 1960. Two of Eckhart's students, Henry Suso and John Tauler, preached extensively and wrote, cautiously perpetuating their master's authentic teaching. Within a generation, the spirituality of the Rhineland Dominicans penetrated even the Franciscan Order and perhaps reached England, where it may have influenced the author of *The Cloud of Unknowing*. After the fourteenth century, references to Eckhart in the chronicles and histories of the Order are couched in terms of respect and honour.

ECKHART'S WRITINGS

Eckhart wrote in both German and Latin, fairly neatly dividing his pastoral and his scholarly works between them. Over 100 German sermons are now recognized as authentic along with four treatises, *The Talks of Instruction (Reden der*

Unterscheidung) he gave to the novices at Erfurt around 1300; a long expanded sermon called *The Nobleman (Von dem edeln Menschen)*; an essay *On Detachment (Von Abgeschiedenheit)*; and *The Book of Divine Consolation (Das Buch der gottlichen Trostung)*, written for Agnes of Hungary, the widowed queen of King Andrew II after the assassination in 1308 of her father, Albert I of Austria, the Emperor-elect.

In addition to some fifty known Latin sermons, a number of fragments of the projected *Opus Tripartitum* survive, as well as the introduction to his commentary on the *Sentences* of Peter Lombard; the *Parisian Questions*, the record of his debates in Paris; a long sermon on the Lord's Prayer; and a number of biblical commentaries, some unfinished.

It is primarily because of his German works that Eckhart is remembered as a spiritual writer and mystic. Most of his sermons were memorized by the nuns in his care and later committed to writing. Their survival may have depended on the ironic fact that they were seized by the Archbishop's inquisitors as evidence, along with other materials.

ECKHART'S WAY

Although considered the 'prince of medieval mystics', or, in Rufus Jones' phrase, 'the peak of the range' of German mystics of the fourteenth century, nothing has survived, if it ever existed, of Eckhart's reflections on his own spirituality, which is typical of Dominicans in the first centuries of the Order's existence. (Eckhart's disciple, Henry Suso, will break dramatically with this tradition with his autobiographical *Life of the Servant*.) Early Dominican spirituality was not self-conscious. Moreover, it is distinguished, like God in Eckhart's way of thinking, by being indistinct – it promotes no particular method such as the Spiritual Exercises of St Ignatius, the Jesus Prayer, or the practices of Teresa of Ávila, much less those of even later spiritualities. What Eckhart would have received as his Dominican legacy is an emphasis on the Truth of the Word, that is, on study leading to contemplation in the widest sense, and that leading to (and from) apostolic activity, specifically preaching.

The 'way' Eckhart proposes, so far as he does so at all, follows the apophatic route of classical Christian contemplation, much as taught by his close contemporary St Gregory Palamas in the East, and practitioners of the *via negativa* in the West, such as the *Cloud* author and Jan van Ruysbroeck. He seems to have taken many of his characteristic themes from issues important to the Beguines. Among them are the Birth of the Word of God in the Soul; the necessity of radical detachment, which is to say, poverty of spirit; the 'darkness' or 'nothingness' of God; and the 'ordinary way' of dis-covering and growing in union with God in the ground of the soul.[3] In his own life and teaching, however, Eckhart was no quietist. For him, as for the Dominican spiritual tradition as a whole, action and contemplation are ultimately one.

UNKNOWING GOD: ECKHART'S NEGATIVE THEOLOGY

As a whole, Eckhart's mystical doctrine centres around the theme of the birth of the Word of God in the souls of the just. In one sermon, he wondered,

> Why do we pray, why do we fast, why do we do all our works, why are we baptised, why (most important of all) did God become man? I would answer, in order that God may be born in the soul and the soul be born in God. For that reason all the scriptures were written, for that reason God created the world and all angelic natures . . .[4]

For Eckhart, as for the ancient mystical theology of the Church, God is uniquely present in the depths of the soul, waiting to break forth into consciousness: 'As surely as the Father in his simple nature bears the Son naturally, just as surely He hears him in the inmost recesses of the spirit, and this is the inner world. Here God's ground is my ground and my ground is God's ground.'[5]

Radically negative in his approach to God-talk (and thinking about God), however, Eckhart maintained that nothing could describe either God or the soul. 'But if God is neither goodness nor being nor truth nor one,' he asks rhetorically, 'what then is He? He is pure nothing: he is neither this nor that. If you think of anything He might be, He is not that.'[6] Further, God 'is beingless [*weselös*] being.'[7] 'God is not being or goodness. Goodness adheres to being and does not go beyond it: for if there were no being there would be no goodness, and being is even purer than goodness. God is not "good", or "better" or "best". Whoever should say God is good would do Him as much injustice as if he called the sun black.'[8]

The Nothingness of God

Talk about 'nothing' and 'nothingness' is notoriously treacherous. Even the most fastidious of philosophical minds occasionally slips into treating them as a 'pseudo-something', as if 'nothing' were capable of description of any kind whatsoever. In the language of the schools, 'nothing' purely and simply *is not*. Non-existence is no more (or less) a predicate than is existence. To say 'There is nothing there', means, and can only mean, that whatever one expected, desired, or feared might or should be there was, in fact, *not* there. One never meets 'a man who wasn't there'.

To say that 'God is nothing' means, and can only mean, that God cannot be included in any way whatsoever in any class of 'things'. God is in no conceivable way a thing among other things. (In the same way, the Aristotelian notion of the 'nothingness of the intellect' means that in respect to all such things, the mind itself cannot be any one of them, else it could not think any of the others. It could not think at all.) But to say, as Eckhart does, that 'creatures are nothing,'[9] does not mean, on the other hand, that they cannot be included in the class of 'things'. It means that, unlike God, in and of themselves such things have no necessary existence. Not only are they totally dependent upon God for their origin and existence, they can either be or not be, as Hamlet understood. It also means that in regard to actual existence, once they were not, that is, they did not in fact exist.

All such language in Eckhart is relative, of course. He is perfectly capable of affirming the dialectical opposite elsewhere: 'God is something and is pure being, and sin is nothing and draws us away from God.'[10] For Eckhart, too, it is only by reconciling the tension between positive and negative statements that it becomes possible to speak meaningfully about God at all. In Eckhart's case, were it not for the huge volume of his theological writings, we might be tempted, as with Wittgenstein and other resolute practitioners of the apophatic way, to take him *too* literally:

> if you want to be without sin and perfect, don't chatter about God. Nor should you (seek to) understand anything about God, for God is above all understanding. One master says: 'If I had a God I could understand, I would no longer consider him God'. So, if you understand anything of Him, that is not He, and by understanding anything of Him you fall into misunderstanding, and from this misunderstanding you fall into brutishness, for whatever in creatures is uncomprehending is brutish. So, if you don't want to become brutish, understand nothing of God the unutterable.[11]

All such negative theology rests on the *biblical* principle that no image is capable of adequately representing God. For Eckhart, the inescapable spiritual consequence, is that we must approach God without images.

> Accordingly a master says, 'To achieve an interior act, a man must collect all his powers as if into a corner of his soul where, hiding away from all images and forms, he can get to work.' Here he must come to a forgetting and an unknowing [*unwizzen*]. There must be a stillness and a silence . . .[12]

Everyone begins, of course, with images and concepts based

on our experience of the world around us and, as Thomas and the long tradition behind him affirm, the biblical tradition itself. But 'For you to know God in God's way, your knowing must become a pure unknowing, and a forgetting of yourself and all creatures.'[13]

This, of course, will become the theme of *The Cloud of Unknowing*. Such 'unknowing', moreover, is not merely a stripping away of concepts (*aphairesis* in the language of the ancient Church), but a stilling of the imagination and the discursive mind, of *thinking*, in order to abide in the conscious presence of the imageless God. Thus, for Eckhart, the truest kind of prayer is wordless awareness, 'in which the soul knows nothing of knowing, wills nothing of loving, and from light it becomes dark.'[14]

This is radical spiritual poverty, a theme Eckhart will expound with daring brilliance in Sermon 52, *'Beati Pauperes Spiritu'*, arguably his most famous and difficult sermon: 'taking poverty in a higher sense, a poor man is one who wants nothing, knows nothing and has nothing.'[15] But it is, in fact, a restatement even there of Eckhart's most characteristic theme, the need for utter detachment from all things in order to 'see' God. But it also introduces us to the mysterious darkness of God.

The Divine Darkness

Thomas Aquinas rarely uses the term 'darkness' (or even 'cloud') for God. Eckhart has no such qualms, particularly in regard to 'unknowing' (*unwizzen*), which leads him to weave together the two strands of mystical discourse: ' . . . the hidden darkness of the eternal light of the eternal Godhead is unknown and shall never be known. And the light of the eternal Father has eternally shone in this darkness, and the darkness does not comprehend the light (John 1:5).'[16]

Like the biblical image of the divine cloud, the divine darkness is, of course, a traditional metaphor, a fact that seems to have escaped the awareness of Eckhart's judges.[17] In language borrowed from both Dionysius and St Thomas, Eckhart says,

> Dionysius [*De mystica theologia* 1] exhorted his pupil Timothy in this sense saying: 'Dear son Timothy, do you with untroubled mind soar above yourself and all your powers, above ratiocination and reasoning, above works, above all modes and existence, into the secret still darkness, that you may come to the knowledge of the unknown super-divine God.' There must be a withdrawal from all things. God scorns to work through images.[18]

Eckhart's Wayless Way: Ordinary Christianity

Eckhart's way thus called for no special practices, heroic penances, pilgrimages, or other 'works'. His apophatic, imageless spirituality remained essentially a 'wayless way', one that (contrary to what some critics aver) is also radically Christological:

> The soul has three ways into God. One is to seek God in all creatures with manifold activity and ardent longing. . . . The second way is a wayless way [*wec âne wec*], free and yet bound, raised, rapt away well-nigh past self and all things, without will and without images, even though not yet in essential being. . . . The third way is called a way, but is really being at home, that is: seeing God without means [*âne mittel*] in His own being. Now Christ says, 'I am the way, the truth and the life' (John 14:16): one Christ as Person, one Christ the Father, one Christ the Spirit, three-in-one: three as way, truth and life, one as the beloved Christ, in which he is all. Outside of this way [*wege*] all creatures circle [around], and are means. But led into God on this way by the light of His Word and embraced by them both in the Holy Spirit – that passes all words.[19]

Eckhart's way is thus characterized, first, by immediacy – 'God works without means and without images, and the freer you are from images, the more receptive you are for His inward working, and the more introverted and self-forgetful, the nearer you are to this.'[20]

Secondly, Eckhart's way, although arduous in its demand for continuous detachment from all concepts of God, is found in the circumstances of ordinary life:

> Indeed, if a man thinks he will get more of God by meditation, by devotion, by ecstasies or by special infusion of grace than by the fireside or in the stable that is nothing but taking God, wrapping a cloak around His head and shoving Him under a bench. For whoever seeks God in a special way gets the way and misses God, who lies hidden in it. But whoever seeks God without any special way gets Him as He is in Himself, and that man lives with the Son, and he is life itself.[21]

In the end, sanctification is God's work, union with God the work of grace, transformation into God the work of divine mercy. Eckhart remained a God-centred mystic, finding all things in God, and God in all things: ' . . . God is unseparated from all things, for God is in all things and is more inwardly in them than they are in themselves.'[22] Thus, Eckhart insists,

> A man may go out into the fields and say his prayers and know God, or he may go to church and know God: but if he is more aware of God because he is in a quiet place, as is usual, that comes from his imperfection and not from God: for God is equally in all things and all places, and is equally ready to give Himself as far as in Him lies: and he knows God rightly who knows God equally (in all things).[23]

ECKHART'S LEGACY

Eckhart's impact on the spiritual life of the women and men of his time and the following decades was diminished but hardly eradicated by the condemnation of fifteen statements torn from his sermons and treatises in 1329. Dominicans who had been his students at Strassburg and Cologne incorporated his doctrine into their preaching and writing, principally among them Henry Suso and John Tauler. He was remembered with affection by the nuns of the southern Rhineland, who had committed his sermons to writing. His memory and teaching also remained alive in the circle of spiritual friends who became known as The Friends of God, including the secular priest, Henry of Nördlingen and the Strassburg merchant, Rulman Merwsin. Towards the end of the century, Eckhart's influence appears in the anonymous *Book of Spiritual Poverty (Das Buch von geistlicher Armuth)*, for a while attributed to Tauler. Hinnebusch points out that

> Tauler's Dominican friend, John of Dambach (d. 1372), borrowed considerably from Eckhart's *Das Buch der gottlichen Trostung* [*Book of Divine Comfort*] in writing his own *Consolatio theologiae*, a book that had considerable impact on the religious life of the late medieval period. Scholars have not determined to what extent Eckhart may have influenced John Ruysbroeck (d. 1381), the eminent Flemish mystic. *The Theologia Deutsch*, written toward the end of the century, though sometimes suspected of pantheism and quietism, actually presented the classical doctrines of the school with little originality, though with more insistence on Christ's mysteries. Cardinal Nicholas of Cusa both read and defended the writings of Eckhart but he thought they ought to 'be removed from general circulation because what he had written for the use and instruction of the educated class was incomprehensible to the common people.' Eckhart's teaching also influenced the writers of the *Devotio moderna*, who incorporated into their works much of his ascetical doctrine.[24]

Echoes of Rhineland mysticism appear also in the writings of the *Cloud* author in England, and in later centuries, Eckhart's influence can be detected in a host of spiritual writers, preachers, theologians, poets, philosophers, artists, and composers (one of the most dramatic sections of John Adams' *Harmonielehre* is entitled 'Meister Eckhart and Quackie'). Eckhart's spiritual influence is greater today than ever before.

CONCLUSION

Insofar as any path or way to God exists for Eckhart, it begins with the *via negativa*, the simplification and unification of consciousness. It has two lanes, so to speak – one is what the early Christians called *aphairesis* – stripping away all ideas, images, and concepts of God so as to rest in Truth, the simple apprehension of God's grounding presence. The other is *apatheia* – the achievement of emotional stability by detachment from all possessiveness, dividedness, and self-centredness, so as to abide in the selfless love of God and neighbour. The rest may not be absolute silence (it certainly was not with Eckhart), but it is the work of mercy and grace, beyond all human worth or effort, God's work.

As a Dominican, Eckhart's commitment to preaching, community life, prayer, and study, was stunningly manifest throughout his entire life. Poverty of Spirit was a leitmotif of his preaching and teaching. He was a tireless promoter of truth, not least in articulating the fundamental realities of our relationship to God. Above all, perhaps, he embodied the characteristic principle of Dominican spirituality that contemplation is not only realized in the midst of active involvement in the world, but perfected in love:

> St Thomas says the active life is better than the contemplative, in so far as in action one pours out for love that which one has gained in contemplation. It is actually the same thing, for we take only from the same ground of contemplation and make it fruitful in works, and thus

the object of contemplation is achieved. Though there is
motion, yet it is all one; it comes from one end, which
is God, and returns to the same, as if I were to go from
one end of this house to the other.... Thus too, in this
activity, we remain in a state of contemplation in God.
The one rests in the other, and perfects the other. For
God's purpose in the union of contemplation is fruitfulness
in works: for in contemplation you serve yourself alone,
but in works of charity you serve the many.[25]

ADDENDUM: ECKHART'S CONDEMNATION

There were many reasons why fifteen propositions taken out
of context from Eckhart's sermons and writings were condemned by the papal commission in 1329, some political, some
historical, some perhaps even personal. But whatever the force
of the combined reasons, what has become increasingly clear
over the past century is that the condemnation was unjust.

At the General Chapter of the Dominican Order held in
Mexico City in 1992, the delegates received the report of a
panel of expert scholars commissioned twelve years before by
the Chapter of Walberberg to review the papal condemnation
with an eye to exonerating Eckhart. After ten years of study,
the panel concluded that Eckhart needed no 'rehabilitation'
in the juridical sense, for neither the Meister himself nor his
doctrine had in fact been condemned. Moreover, the bull itself
was officially restricted to the Archdiocese of Cologne.[26] On the
basis of these findings, in March 1992, the Master of the Order
at that time, Fr Damian Byrne, formally requested Cardinal
Joseph Ratzinger to abrogate the bull of condemnation.

While this has not yet occurred, it is worth noting that Pope
John Paul II in an audience of September 1985 (quoted in
L'Osservatore Romano, 28 October 1985) remarked,

> Did not Eckhart teach his disciples: 'All that God asks you
> most pressingly is to go out of yourself ... and let God be
> God in you?' One could think that in separating himself

from creatures, the mystic leaves his brothers, humanity, behind. The same Eckhart affirms that, on the contrary, the mystic is marvellously present to them on the only level where he can truly reach them, that is, in God.[27]

6. CATHERINE OF SIENA: THE MYSTIC IN ACTION

The prophet is but the mystic in control of the forces of history, declaring their necessary outcome: the mystic in action is the prophet. In the prophet, the cognitive certainty of the mystic becomes historic and particular; and this is the necessary destiny of that certainty: mystic experience must complete itself in prophetic consciousness.

William Ernest Hocking,
The Meaning of God in Human Experience[1]

Prophets not only go frequently without honour in their own land, they often come to a bad end at the hands of their countrymen. But eventual failure, even martyrdom, do not invalidate the prophet's vocation or achievement. They may even prove them. In any case, whether or not one agrees with Rudolf Bell that Catherine of Siena ended her days a pathetic failure suffering from delusions of grandeur, it is hard to question her role as a prophet as energetic and effective as Deborah, Gael, Judith, or Esther.[2]

Catherine also ranks as one of the great mystics of the Church, not only for her spiritual doctrine, but for her visions and revelations and those emblematic and extraordinary experiences of progressive union with God – mystical espousal, the exchange of hearts with Christ, the stigmata – which the world perhaps too easily identifies with the mystical life.[3] Even so, ordinary women and men have been drawn to her as much for her charm, vitality, and common sense as any signs and wonders.

Catherine's love for the Order of Preachers, particularly her support for the reform movement of the late Middle Ages, justly earned her the reputation as its second founder. In this, she greatly resembles that other remarkable saint, mystic, spiritual writer, and Carmelite reformer, Teresa of Ávila, alongside whom she was declared a Doctor of the Church by Pope Paul VI in 1970.

Also like Teresa, Catherine was not a dogmatic theologian. We will not find in her writings distinctions between apophatic and kataphatic discourse or disquisitions on the unknowability of God. She is a contemplative in action and a spiritual writer of astonishing insight and energy dispensing advice and encouragement to a wild variety of correspondents, from peasants to popes. Yet as she was a Dominican, one of the greatest of all, it is worth inquiring whether those character-istic doctrines of her great brother teachers (and mystics) are found also in her message.

LIFE IN ABUNDANCE

Like the father of Francis of Assisi, Giacomo Benincasa was a dyer. He and his wife, Lapa Piagenti, had a large family. Catherine, the youngest of twenty-five children, was born about 1347. (Giovanna, her twin, died shortly after their birth.) When she was six, Catherine saw her first vision of Christ in the sky over the nearby Dominican priory. A year later, she pledged herself to perpetual virginity. In 1362 she renewed her resolve not to marry after the death of her sister Bonaven-tura, who had encouraged her to improve her appearance with that end in view. And, at the advice of her cousin, a young Dominican friar, she drastically cut her hair. Mona Lapa's strenuous efforts to force her to change her mind went unavailing.

Around 1363, Catherine joined the *Mantellate* – a group of laywomen, most of them elderly widows, associated with the Dominican Order. By the age of eighteen, she had overcome all resistance to her plans. Her father allowed her a room of her own in the attic, where Catherine undertook a life of seclusion, asceticism, and prayer.

Transformation in Christ

In this mystical cocoon, Catherine underwent a series of experiences culminating about three years later, following her father's death, in a second transformation. After experiencing a vision in which Christ espoused himself to her and commissioned her to carry his love to the whole world, she emerged from her seclusion and began to tend the poor and wretched of Siena. But her ministry quickly took her beyond the lepers, plague victims, poor, sick, and homeless citizens of her native town, and she began addressing her considerable energies to peace-making among warring Italian cities, correcting abuses of power and privilege, reforming the Dominican Order, and even restoring the papacy to Rome.

In 1370, Catherine, now twenty-three, experienced an exchange of hearts with Jesus, who said, 'See, dearest daughter, a few days ago I took your heart from you; now, in the same way, I give you my own heart. For the future, it is by [this heart] that you must live.'[4]

Mystic in the Marketplace

For four years, Catherine continued caring for the sick and destitute. A band of disciples began developing around her. Made up of lay women and men, Dominicans, diocesan priests, and even members of the aristocracy, they saw themselves as a spiritual family and referred to her as 'Mother'. It was at this time that Catherine more or less miraculously learned to read and began to dictate a torrent of letters. Among her goals was a new Crusade to free the Holy Land, and, incidentally, reunite Christendom.

In 1374, the Master of the Order became concerned about the growing reputation of the young Sienese lay Dominican woman as a spiritual guide, reformer, and visionary. Summoned to the general chapter of the Order meeting at Florence, Catherine was examined carefully. Exonerated, she returned to Siena, although the chapter assigned Raymond of Capua, a skilled theologian and administrator, to serve as spiritual director to her and her followers. Raymond's initial doubts about the genuineness of her visions and her mission were soon dispelled, and he became as much her disciple as her guide.

Confronting Princes and Powers: the Stigmata

Catherine was not to remain in Siena. After visiting the tomb of St Agnes of Montepulciano, the first Dominican woman to be canonized, she embarked upon a strenuous series of missions for Florence and other cities as diplomat and peacemaker. In Pisa in 1375, while praying in the Church of St Christina, Catherine received the stigmata, which, at her request, remained invisible until after her death.

The following year, Catherine and her followers journeyed to the papal court to plead with Pope Gregory XI on behalf of Florence, which had taken up arms against the papal forces and was placed under interdict. Since 1305, except for a brief period between 1367–70, the papacy had resided at Avignon, where weak French popes were controlled with little difficulty by strong French kings. Catherine took advantage of the occasion to persuade the Pope to return to Rome and end the 'Babylonian captivity' of the Church. Despite the pleas of his family, the opposition of the French cardinals, the will of the king, and the advice of his councillors, Gregory did as Catherine (and others) bade him.

After a harrowing journey, the Pope solemnly entered Rome in January, 1377. Unhappy in that squalid and volatile city, however, within a year Gregory was planning to return to Avignon when he suddenly died. The Roman populace demanded an Italian pope. Terrified of the mob, the cardinals elected the Archbishop of Bari as Urban VI, the first non-French pope in sixty years. Urban was impulsive, violent, and mentally unstable. After four months of aggravation, the French cardinals fled Rome, nullified Urban's election on the grounds of duress, and elected Robert of Geneva as Clement VI. At least as brutal as Urban, the antipope was not mad, however, and established his pontificate at Avignon. The Great Western Schism had begun.

Reforming the Church: Catherine the Prophet and Preacher

Catherine, who had returned to her birthplace at the end of 1376, supported Urban VI despite his excesses, for she – more clearly than many – was able to perceive the difference between the office and the man. Regardless of Urban's manifest failings, he was the legitimate pope. She completed her masterwork, *The Dialogue*. Then Catherine began dictating a stream of letters – to Urban himself, to the cardinals, bishops, to the nobility and clergy of Europe. In 1378, Urban summoned her to Rome, where Catherine would devote the remaining eighteen months of her life to defending his papacy and labouring to restore the unity of the Church.

She wrote, preached, prayed, and pushed herself beyond the limits of even her formidable energies. At last, having failed to reconcile Urban and his opponents, she fell seriously ill, unable (or unwilling) to eat or drink. For two months she lay paralyzed. Then, on 29 April 1380, she died, surrounded by her disciples and calling on the mercy of the Blood of Jesus.

One of the most gifted and extraordinary women of any era, Catherine was canonized in 1461. In 1939, Pope Pius XII declared her with St Francis of Assisi co-patron of Italy. And in 1970, she and St Teresa of Ávila, whose life and achievements so greatly resembled hers, were declared the first women Doctors of the Church by Pope Paul VI.

CATHERINE'S WRITINGS

Despite her inability to read or write for much of her life, Catherine's literary productivity is amazing by any standards. Of the extant materials preserved by her disciples and correspondents, there are 382 letters, the *Book of Divine Providence*, more commonly known as *The Dialogue*, and twenty-six long prayers recorded by her disciples while she was in ecstasy.

In addition to Catherine's own writings, the major sources include the *Life* (or *Major Legend*) written by Raymond of Capua; the depositions of twenty-three witnesses at Venice during the process of canonization from 1411–16; and the *Minor Legend* and *Supplement* to Raymond's *Life* by Tommaso Caffarini. To these may be added several small works emanating from the circle of Catherine's disciples, including *The Treatise on Consummate Perfection*.[5]

CATHERINE'S SPIRITUALITY

Catherine's life and teaching focused on the overwhelming immensity of God's love for all creation; the redeeming passion and death of Jesus, the Incarnate Truth, the Bridge between God and humanity, and the ardent Lover of the soul; and the response of self-transcending love by God's friends, expressed in the service of truth and justice, particularly towards the poor and suffering.

One of the richest sources of Catherine's spirituality can be found in her letters, where she expounds on her favourite themes, such as drowning in the Sea of God's Being and cutting out the root of self-love with the knife of self-hatred. Catherine delights in piling image upon image; the Well of the Soul, the Cell of Self-Knowledge, Christ the Bridge. 'There is no blood without fire, nor fire without blood,' she writes vehemently.[6] Or as in one of her allegories, she apostrophizes with densely layered exuberance, 'O sweet Lamb roasted by the fire of divine charity on the stake of the cross!'[7]

There is a sufficient wealth of motif in Catherine's spirituality to fill volumes. Of particular interest is her emphasis on the knowledge and love of God attained through 'self-noughting', as the *Cloud* author has it, the realization of creaturely 'nothingness' and the awareness that God is All. Here, Catherine's chosen expressions tend initially toward the dark and frightening – violence, death, even murder, only to rise exultantly in images of light and dazzling vibrancy. Her sense of the dramatic is unparalleled in mystical literature.

Unlearned Learner

Even by the standards of her own time, Catherine was no scholar. Formally she was an uneducated laywoman, illiterate at the time of her profession as a Mantellata, yet one whose capacity for learning was astonishing. In most respects, she was self-taught, although the presence in her circle of learned Dominicans such as Raymond of Capua provided her major opportunities to deepen her understanding of Scripture and theology. She was, needless to say, an attentive auditor, not least of sermons. But Catherine also learned to read. Noffke writes,

> she told Raimondo da Capua that she 'had resolved to learn to read in order to be able to recite the praises of God and the Hours of the Office.' In any case, she engaged her friend Alessa de' Saracini to teach her, and did master the art enough to be able to read what she wanted to. (There is a fair probability that she later learned to write, at least in a very elementary way.)[8]

The influences of a variety of sources on Catherine's teachings have been proposed (and denied) by scholars. In addition to the Bible, Noffke holds that she shows the influence of a number of theological and spiritual writers, among them Augustine, John Cassian, Gregory the Great, Bernard of Clairvaux, Francis of Assisi, Thomas Aquinas, Ubertino da Casale, Passavanti, Dominic Cavalca, and Colombini. 'Like everything that came her way she absorbed them all and integrated them into her whole knowledge. Theologically there is nothing new or original.'⁹

Catherine's spiritual doctrine is *all* her doctrine. As with Eckhart, at the heart of her teaching lies the central fact of human history, the saving presence among us of God Incarnate. As one student has recently pointed out,

> [Caroline Walker] Bynum has suggested that for Catherine the incarnation, not the resurrection, was the centre of her theology, and that this was connected with her understanding of Christ's taking on of human bodiliness in order to feed and save the world.¹⁰

DOCTOR OF DIVINITY: CATHERINE THE TEACHER

While Catherine cannot be called a Thomist, nor does she show the slightest influence of the Rhineland mystics, her teaching shares with them and Thomas several characteristic themes which can be described as Dominican in as much as they typify a characteristic approach to the spiritual life.

Knowing God: The One Who Is

The negative element found in Thomas and Eckhart, is also reflected in Catherine's teaching. More kataphatic in her approach than either of her Dominican brethren, her teaching stops far short of any notion of the divine nothingness or the paradoxical and reciprocal nothingness of creature and Creator that permeates Eckhart's sermons and treatises. Nor does she allude to the unknowability of God even in terms favoured by Thomas. However, insight into her own nothingness in comparison to the infinite sea of God's being is foundational. It leads to her exaltation of holy desire as the path towards union with God through contemplative vision and especially by way of eradicating self-will, much as Thomas and Eckhart insist.

Commenting on one of Catherine's creative images, Giuliana

Cavallini demonstrates the ease with which she moves from an awareness of mystical nothingness to total immersion in both God and the abyss of the soul, as simple a step for her as it had been for the Meister, for whom God's ground and the soul's ground were one:

> [The soul] is a well which has water and earth within it. We know our misery in the earth. We realize that we are nothing. Since we are 'not,' we see that our being is from God. O ineffable burning charity, I see that earth and living waters are found here, that is, true knowledge of his sweet and true will that wants nothing other than our sanctification. We, therefore, enter into the depths of this well, dwelling within and knowing ourselves and the goodness of God.[11]

Catherine's profound awareness of her own absolute dependence on God arose early in her spiritual life, as she later told Raymond. In one of the most quoted passages from her *Life*, she relates how God said to her, 'Do you know, daughter, who you are and who I am? If you know these two things you have beatitude in your grasp. You are she who is not, and *I am the One Who is*. Let your soul be penetrated with this truth, and the Enemy can never lead you astray.'[12]

Such a vision is not without contemporary relevance. In the still sober light of the devastation of the Second World War, Charles Journet applied and extended Catherine's fundamental insight in terms that still speak eloquently at the end of a century of terrible wars:

> Yes, I am he who is not. And these things about me: the sweetness of the air, the scent of roses, all these things that I love; and the anguish and the grief, so many lovely things, so many sad things, all these ravished lives and homelands, so many crimes, so many blasphemies, so many horrors – these things are not nothing; they are real; and yet there is always one point of view from which it is true to say that they are not. It is rigorously true to

say that, in the manner in which God is, they are not. The peace that the understanding of this gives is inexpressible. And this knowledge measures the abyss which separates the level on which the problem of evil binds us, from the infinite height whence it is seen to be resolved.[13]

Such knowledge gives not only peace, but also love, a love that breaks through the immobilizing pessimism that results from trying to confront immense evil without the support of something more powerful, more Real. Cavallini comments,

> The knowledge of these two extremes – 'I am He Who is, you are she who is not' – is wonderfully grounded in the incarnation of the Word for our salvation. It does not remain a cold, abstract concept, but is translated into love; rather, the double name of hatred-love: love for God, hatred for everything that separates from God. Therefore, the well water is a living water: the driving force of our wills. This water is the knowledge of God's will that wants us to be saints and why he gave himself for our sanctification.[14]

If sin, evil, and the threat of annihilation challenge us today as they have in the past, including Catherine's past, love is the answer, as Julian of Norwich would say in similar fashion later that century. In some respects, it is the only answer: 'This sweet fire has not ended nor will it ever end. If his affection for us would come to an end, we would cease, for the being that he gave us would end. Only the fire of love moves him to draw us to himself.'[15]

Here, Catherine is also not far from Eckhart in her grasp of the essential nothingness of the creature in relation to God, for the Meister himself had said, 'All creatures are pure nothing. I do not say they are a trifle or they are anything: they are pure nothing. What has no being, is not. All creatures have no being, for their being consists in the presence of God. If God turned away for an instant from all creatures, they would perish.'[16] For Eckhart the nothingness of the self and the Nothingness of God are dialectically reciprocal. Truth, for Catherine, entails the felt realization that her nothingness is the arena of God's manifestation, the 'place', as Eckhart would say, once evacuated, where God 'works'.

'But,' Noffke asks in regard to Catherine's ecstatic self-abasement before the sovereign Being of God, 'isn't this the sort of self-denigrating humility we moderns have put aside for a more affirming, positive view of ourselves as God's creation?' 'No,' she replies,

> not if we see it as Catherine saw it. 'We must recognize the truth in everything,' she writes to Queen Giovanna of Naples. 'I mean, we must love in God and for God's sake everything that has being, because God is Truth itself, and without God nothing has being.' [Letter T317.] This is why God says that Catherine 'is not': Catherine's being is totally dependent upon God. Catherine of herself is not; when Catherine does what is not of God, she does 'that which is not' – she sins. But as creature of God, it is in the very being of God, in the very truth of God, that Catherine shares. So she calls God 'the gentle Master of truth, who is the maker and giver of everything that is.'[17]

Poverty of Spirit: Detachment for the Sake of Love

Common to Thomas and Eckhart, and found in the teaching of the Beguines and the *Cloud* author as well, poverty of will or, in Catherine's more violent metaphor, 'killing our self-will', is another major motif of her doctrine. That spiritual transformation entails conforming our recalcitrant will to that of God rather than somehow obliterating it or suppressing desire is, of course, her meaning, as it was of the Beguines, Thomas, and Eckhart. But the exertion remains not only violent, but costly. God says, 'Your selfish will must in every-thing be slain, drowned, subjected to my will.'[18]

For Catherine, as for the *Cloud* author, such 'self-noughting' is also the necessary condition for the possibility of true self-understanding, which is to say, the awareness of our total dependence on God and God's love. It is a stage in the ecstatic emancipation from the self-centredness that cripples personal growth and frustrates the turn towards others in love. Catherine writes,

> When the soul considers and sees the great excellence and strength of the fire of the Holy Spirit within herself, she is inebriated, and knowing her creator's love she completely surrenders herself. Living, she is dead and feels within herself neither love nor pleasure for creatures, since the memory is already filled with the affection of her creator. The understanding seeks neither to understand nor see any created thing separate from God. It understands and sees herself only as non-being, and the goodness of God within herself. She sees that infinite goodness wants nothing but her good. Then her love towards God has become perfect; since she has nothing within herself, she cannot hold to the rapid race of desire, but runs without any weight or chain.[19]

Self-drowned in the Sea of God's Being, the soul is drained of self, then replenished with new life, new love, new desire, and a divine delight in creation. Noffke writes, '... God speaks ... of the vessel of our heart being "filled with the sea that is my very self, the most high eternal Godhead." And, being filled with the sea, it overflows in charity, "and so," Catherine writes, "I weep with those who weep and rejoice with those who rejoice." '[20]

Being filled with God's own love, its outreach towards others in compassionate service is irresistible: 'the love a soul sees that God has for her, she in turn extends to all creatures. She immediately feels compelled to love her neighbor as herself for she sees how fully she herself is loved by God when she beholds herself in her source, the sea of God's being. She then desires to love herself in God and God in herself.'[21]

Far from extinguishing passion, immersion in God purifies and inflames it. In one of her characteristic images, Catherine thus writes, '[One should never cease] putting the wood of self-knowledge on the fire of holy desire. These are the logs that nourish the fire of divine charity . . . uniting the soul with its neighbor. The more one gives fuel to the fire (that is, the word of self-knowledge) so much more increases the warmth of love for Christ and one's neighbor.'[22]

At the end of the day, all great spiritual teachers seem to agree that involved self-absorption, whether called narcissism or pride, is the supreme obstacle to self-knowledge, the perception of God's pervading presence, and especially the ability to turn to others in compassion and justice. That was certainly Catherine's understanding and it connects her intrinsically with the tradition she adopted and renewed.

CATHERINE'S ABIDING INFLUENCE

Catherine's impact on her world was immediate and mixed. Often the focus of controversy, some of her diplomatic interventions failed utterly, others were highly successful. Noffke comments,

> Historically, Catherine has sometimes been given more credit than she is due for her influence in the great political crises of her day. Though she almost certainly exerted the final pressure that activated Pope Gregory XI's resolve to move the papacy back from Avignon to Rome in 1376, those who blamed her for the schism that followed on that move may not be entirely mistaken. In her zeal for the unity of the Church she did sometimes stand, rightly or wrongly, intransigent on the politically catastrophic side of a specific question (at least as we see it now in retrospect). . . . Catherine's more significantly positive contribution to questions of social and political justice lies, I believe, in her attempts to influence individuals whose primary responsibilities were political and social. Of the 382 letters that survive of Catherine's correspondence, 67 are addressed to political figures: 13 to

kings and queens, 38 to lesser civic officials, 10 to lawyers, and 6 to military leaders.[23]

Catherine is mainly remembered, and always will be, as one of the greatest mystics and spiritual writers of all time. But even as a spiritual figure, she was often the target of suspicion, resentment, and hostility, not unlike the prophetic paradigm anywhere. But among those who knew her best, she was 'Mamma', the wise woman (despite her relative youth). The world claims her, but through her writings and the further work of her immediate disciples, she especially exercised a lasting influence on the reform movement in the Dominican Order, including the efforts of John Dominici, Jerome Savona-rola, and Catherine dei Ricci, right down to our own time.

MOTHER OF DOMINICANS

Not without reason is Catherine considered the second founder of the Order. Through letters, conferences, and spiritual direction addressed to friars, nuns, and tertiaries, she continually returned to the characteristic themes of Dominican spirituality – preaching, community life, prayer, and study; poverty of spirit; the primacy of Truth; and contemplation expressed in active ministry.

First of all, her commitment to the constitutive elements of Dominican life is seen in her own example as well as her constant exhortations to her Dominican entourage to fulfil the ideal of their vocation. Here, surely, is the heart of her contribution to the movement of reform in the Order.

Truth, God's truth, lies close to the heart of all Catherine's writings and, indeed, her life as a whole. Noffke writes,

> At the base of all of Catherine's thinking about justice is 'God's truth.' And God's truth is this: that God wants only our good, our fulfillment in truth and love, our holiness within God's own holiness. If we recognize that truth and act accordingly, we are 'judging (or discerning) God's will justly.'[24]

'Cry out as if you had a million voices,' she urges. 'It is silence which kills the world.'[25] 'Proclaim the truth and do not be silent through fear.'[26]

Spiritual poverty was expressed for Catherine, as we have seen abundantly, in her constant insistence on the need for detachment from self-will. Profoundly contemplative throughout her life, Catherine felt drawn to its monastic expression and saw to the foundation of several communities of nuns. But her own ministry was in the 'marketplace', the public forum where the fruit of her own contemplation was expressed in preaching, whether by pen or by the living word itself. 'In the devastation surrounding her, Catherine's own Dominican call inspired her to focus on the fire and zeal of apostolic preaching as a means of Church reform. Raymond writes of more than a thousand people often "crowding in from the mountains and the country districts around Siena just to see her and hear her." '[27]

'Bear God's word with fire!' she wrote to him when he faltered on one of his missions. 'Pour out the truth, sow the seed of God's word everywhere!'[28]

The Call of Love

Not only did Catherine teach that love, especially the self-transcending love that impels a person to lay down her life for her friends, occupied the summit of the mystical ascent, she demonstrated it throughout her life, from the service she rendered in the dreadful hospitals of Siena, tending to those no one else would bother with, to what amounts to her self-offering out of love for the unity of the Church at the end of her short life. Today it is easy, perhaps much too easy, to read into Catherine's sacrificial mysticism the consequences of low self-esteem absorbed from her early struggles with her parents and the continual opposition she encountered because of her gender.

That Catherine was scarred psychologically from her struggles against parental and societal bias may be freely admitted. But to describe her mission and indeed her life-work as ultimately flawed and in fact a failure, as does Rudolf Bell, ignores the plain evidence of her writing, her impact on both Church and state, and the lasting impression she made not only on her closest companions, but on the whole world. If Catherine suffered from anorexia nervosa, it was in a form vastly different from that which afflicts young women in the late twentieth century. But perhaps even here, she provides an example, not one to imitate so much as to learn from.[29]

CONCLUSION: CATHERINE AND HER MISSION

Using the metaphor of losing and recovering one's voice, Carol Gilligan, Patricia Killen, and other writers situate the discussion of women's role in the Church within the context of speech, which is especially appropriate for theology.[30] But concentrating on discourse can accidentally overlook the place of action, which is to say, active ministry apart from teaching and, indeed, preaching, the two areas which, along with officiating at the Eucharist and the major sacraments, have been barred to women most frequently by reason of their gender. Even so, it is precisely in the area of ministry (including teaching and preaching) that churchwomen have distinguished themselves, often in extraordinary ways. Thus Catherine achieved distinction as a diplomat, mystic, and Doctor of the Church. But also in her care for the poor, sick, and suffering, which surpassed even that of Francis of Assisi, himself no priest, the ministry of the young Dominican lay woman, Catherine of Siena, revealed the hand of God powerfully at work. As Antonia Lacey observes,

> If empowerment is considered to be a marker of an outgoing and active Christianity, one that elucidates and in some way changes people in their relationship to each other and to God, then it is clearly possible to argue that Catherine was so empowered. However, it would be wrong to attribute to Catherine, in her particular situation, the

psychological insights of the twentieth century and to read into her life a knowing challenge of the structures of patriarchy under which she lived. Rather, her empowerment stems from her affective and contemplative life, in which she experiences herself as united to God, and from her absolute belief that it is God who has commanded her to act, and that God in fact works through her.[31]

7. BEYOND THE WAYLESS WAY

Thomas, Eckhart, and Catherine shine with unique and exceptional brilliance within the main sequence of the Dominican spiritual tradition, representing characteristic ways of knowing and unknowing God in contemplative, prophetic ministry. But they are accompanied, before and after, by a host of companions who follow, at least in the beginning, similar pathways.

Eckhart's followers, collectively but not exclusively known as 'the Friends of God', are largely found in the Rhineland. Although his (and their) influence spreads in wider and wider circles as time passes, it also diminishes in force. Catherine stimulates a reform movement rooted in the mystical awareness of God's incomprehensible Presence that survives the disruptions of the Great Western Schism and, particularly in Italy, flowers during the Renaissance in the seemingly disparate forms of painting and prophetic preaching. The influence of Thomas, adopted as the common teacher of the Order, radiates broadly enough to figure in all these areas – from the sermons of Tauler to the portraits of Fra Angelico, as well as the thundering denunciations of that great and doomed preacher, Savonarola, and the idealistic and humanitarian political doctrine of Vitoria and Las Casas, right down to our own time.[1]

GOD'S FRIENDS

In addition to the hundreds of Beguine houses, many of the congregations to whom Eckhart, Suso, Tauler, and their confrères preached were convents of enclosed Dominican nuns, a great flowering of which had erupted in the Rhineland at this time. Although associated with the 'Sisters Preachers' from the inception of the Order, the friars were officially charged by papal order in 1267 with the spiritual guidance of the nuns, specifically by supplying preachers and confessors. The Teutonic province (and after the division of 1303, both provinces of Teutonia and Saxony) complied by assigning gifted and eloquent friars, many of whom, from Albert to Tauler and his companions, were infused with a deeply mystical sense of God.[2] Frequently, the mystical teaching of the Rhineland Dominicans was a collaborative effort between the nuns (or Beguines) and friars, such as Henry of Halle and Mechthild of Magdeburg, Peter of Dacia and Christine of Stommeln, Margaret Ebner and the secular priest, Henry von Nördlingen, and especially in the case of Elsbet Stagl, Prioress of Töss, and Bl. Henry Suso.[3]

Among the outstanding Dominican spiritual writers and teachers involved in the ministry to the nuns and Beguines were several contemporaries of Eckhart, some (but not all) of whom were influenced by the lofty Neoplatonic-hued spirituality of negation and transcendence associated with the school of Albert the Great. Among the exceptions was Eckhart's lector and defender at Cologne, Nicholas of Strassburg, whose approach was indebted to Thomas and more focally centred on the figure of Christ.[4] Gerard and John Korngin, brothers from Sterngassen, were similarly more drawn to Thomas rather than Eckhart's Dionysian way. But the main lines of Eckhart's spiritual doctrine were clearly and eloquently adopted by his two most celebrated students, Henry Suso and John Tauler, who combined fidelity to the memory of their Meister with originality and depth.

Although recent scholarship has exonerated Eckhart of doctrinal misprision, and his teaching has been commended even by Pope John Paul II, the shadow of the condemnation of 1329 has clouded many treatments of Rhineland spirituality. The conventional 'received tradition' regarding Henry Suso and

John Tauler holds that they 'utilized' elements of Eckhart's doctrine, but 'purged' it of its more extreme and even heretical aspects or simply 'distanced' themselves from certain teachings. It could be just as accurately claimed that they perpetuated Eckhart's most characteristic teachings, nuancing them carefully to emphasize their orthodox intention, if also reducing the force of his creative and often hair-raising expression. Nowhere, however, does Suso or Tauler explicitly 'correct' Eckhart's teaching, much less repudiate it, even, as was the case with Ruysbroeck, while essentially repeating it.

Undoubtedly, both of Eckhart's major 'disciples' gained a wide and enthusiastic following by their own merits as preachers and writers. Tauler's works were enormously popular and were translated into many languages. Suso became one of the favourite writers of the Middle Ages.[5] But, like Eckhart, both Suso and Tauler became suspect because of their emphasis on faith over works, especially in Tauler's case, whose teaching greatly influenced Luther on his way to the Reformation. In 1330, one year after the papal bull condemning fragments of Eckhart's teaching was published, Suso was removed from office as lector of his priory and censured by the General Chapter of Maastricht, ostensibly for his spirited defence of his teacher. But his and Tauler's mystical appeal also earned them the opprobrium of later censors such as the stern Everard Mercurian, who in the sixteenth century proscribed their use by members of the fledgling Society of Jesus.[6]

The Ebullient Servant

Henry Suso was known even in his own time for his charm and sincerity as well as the elegance of his language, steeped as it was in the romantic literature of Swabia. Early on, his classmates attached the nickname 'Amandus' to him, which is almost untranslatable into English but brings to mind a phrase young Americans use in regard to amiable but sometimes exasperating friends: 'You gotta love him.'[7]

Among the characteristic themes Suso shares with Eckhart's teaching are the birth of God in the soul and the Divine Darkness and Nothingness. In *The Little Book of Truth*, he writes, obscurely enough,

> The *disciple* began anew to inquire and said: Tell me, what do you call the manner in which a person attains his blessedness?
>
> Response: One can call it a giving birth, as is written in the gospel of St John that he gave the power and capacity to become God's Son to all those who are born of nothing else than of God. . . . I shall tell you still more. Unless a person is conscious of two contraries, that is, two things that contradict each other, seeing them as one with each other, then certainly without a doubt it is not at all easy to talk to him about such things. . . .
>
> Question: What are these contraries?
>
> Answer: An eternal nothing and its coming to be in time.
>
> Objection: Two contraries existing as one in any manner contradicts every branch of knowledge.
>
> Answer: You and I do not meet on one branch or in one place. You make your way along one path and I along another. Your questions arise from human thinking, and I respond from a knowledge that is far beyond all human comprehension. You must give up human understanding if you want to reach the goal, because the truth is known by not knowing.[8]

Such admittedly tame intimations of the apophatic discourse that shocked Eckhart's judges (and probably his listeners) are amplified, however, in Suso's *Life of the Servant*, transcribed by Elsbet Stagl:

> This naked unity [of the Godhead] is a dark stillness and a restful calm that no one can understand but one into whom unity has shined with its essence. . . . [In God the human spirit] is stripped and bared of all limited modes

of being in the simple divine being that has no limited modes. This illumines for itself all things in simple stillness. Here the remaining distinction of Persons according to their individuality is disregarded in a simplicity that excludes modes of being. . . . This same spiritual 'where' previously mentioned, where a tried and true servant should dwell with the eternal Son, one can call the nameless existing nothingness. Here the spirit encounters the nothing of unity. This unity is called a 'nothing' because the spirit can find no human manner of saying what it is. Instead, the spirit clearly feels that it is being preserved by something other than itself. Therefore, what is preserving it is more properly a something than a nothing, but for the (human) spirit it is rather a nothing according to how it exists.[9]

Here, all the familiar themes are layered in a dense, lapidary fashion that must have been bewildering in one who was known for his charm, sweetness, and elegance of expression rather than metaphysical interests:

This [divine mode of] knowledge . . . sets the spirit apart (from itself). This happens in the nothing of unity in accordance with the unfathomable knowledge that the nothing has. The spirit loses its own knowledge because it loses itself, lacking any awareness of self and forgetting all things. And this happened when the spirit in itself turned away from the created nature of its self and all things toward the naked uncreatedness of nothingness.[10]

Doctor Tauler

In his sermons and writings, John Tauler, too, echoes the familiar themes of the birth of God in the soul, knowing and unknowing, and the dark nothingness of God. Much like Suso, Tauler devoted most of his career as a preacher to the care of large numbers of Beguines and Dominican nuns, but also developed a sizable following of lay people.[11] Many of his

sermons and conferences, like Eckhart's, were copied down
and preserved. Also as with Eckhart, others were added to
these collections that were not his own, including some of
the Meister's. Because of his widespread popularity, Tauler's
sermons and conferences remained part of the Protestant heri-
tage despite their manifest Catholic provenance.

In a sermon for the Monday before Palm Sunday, Tauler
said, in true Eckhartian fashion,

> Whoever arrives here has discovered what he has been
> searching for far and wide. His spirit will be led into a
> hidden desert far beyond his natural faculties. Words
> cannot describe it, for it is the unfathomable darkness
> where the divine Goodness reigns above all distinctions.
> And the soul is led further, into the oneness of God's simple
> unity, so that it loses the ability to draw any distinctions
> between the object and its own emotions. For in this unity
> all multiplicity is lost; it is the unity which unifies multi-
> plicity.
>
> . . . No one can understand these distinctions better than
> those who have gone beyond distinctions and have
> attained unity. This state is called and indeed is an unfath-
> omable darkness, and yet it is the essential light. It is and
> is said to be an incomprehensible and solitary wilderness,
> for no one can find his way there, for it is above all ways,
> above all modes and manners.[12]

Elsewhere, in a passage both dense and eloquent, Tauler
not only appeals to the Dionysian tradition, connecting the
divine darkness with love, although differently than does, for
instance, the *Cloud* author, but also gives it a distinctively
kenotic and Christological interpretation:

> Now I will speak of another love, and it is as high above the
> first as Heaven is above earth. . . . Whoever could attain to
> this love would have attained a lofty peak indeed. Here
> the self is left far behind; and instead of fullness there is
> emptiness. Not Knowledge, but non-Knowledge prevails

now; for that love is beyond all modes and manners. . . .
So entirely stripped must it be of self that this very self
eludes its glance. Neither thought nor desire can it harbor.
It cannot even sacrifice this poverty to God, for in its non-
Knowledge it cleaves closely to it. It must deny its very
self, and die to all sensible images which it possessed in
the first stage, in order to enter that realm where God
loves Himself and is His own object of love. In this
denuding of ourselves we are reformed in the form of God,
clothed with His divinity. It is the hidden darkness of
which Saint Dionysius spoke.[13]

Despite the vicissitudes of approbation and reprobation at the
hands of later authorities, the spiritual doctrine of Eckhart's
two most illustrious disciples remained influential in the Dominican Order and beyond for several centuries. Hinnebusch
writes,

Their ideas reached the Dominicans Venturino of Bergamo
and Louis Chardon, the Carmelites John of St Samson,
John of the Cross, and Teresa of Ávila, the Jesuit Peter
Canisius, the Capuchin Benet of Canfield, the Benedic-
tines John of Castel and Louis of Blois, the Carthusians
Dionysius of Rijckel, Ludolph of Saxony, and Lawrence
Surius, the Spanish Franciscan John of the Angels, the
Passionist founder [Paul] of the Cross, the seventeenth-
century German Pietists, and the writers of the eight-
eenth century French School of Spirituality.[14]

THE WIDER SPHERE

While negative theology and an emphasis on unknowing was
a motif of the circle of Eckhart's disciples, it was by no means
restricted to the Dominican Order nor even characteristic of
many of its later spiritual writers.[15] A number of influential
works appeared at this time, some of them influenced by the
Dominican Rhineland tradition, but others arose independently. (In some cases it is not easy to differentiate.) Among the

non-Dominican German works that perpetuated Eckhartian themes were the writings of Rulman Merswin, the *Theologia Germanica*, and *The Book of Spiritual Poverty* (although this may have been composed by a Dominican disciple of Tauler). Outside of Germany, *The Cloud of Unknowing* with its companion works and the writings of Jan van Ruysbroeck manifest a strong Dionysian tone with more or less characteristic Dominican aspects. In the following century, the writings of Cardinal Nicholas of Cusa reflect often the Rhineland thematic, although intentionally departing from Eckhart's teaching in several respects.

God's Banker

Rulman Merswin (1307–82) was a rich banker of Strassburg who attached himself to Tauler until the latter's death in 1360.[16] After experiencing a religious conversion, Merswin and his wife devoted their lives and fortune to the establishment and direction of a retreat centre for priests and lay people called The Green Isle. In years to come, Merswin became the self-styled leader of the Friends of God. After his death, a collection of letters were discovered among his possessions including a group purporting to come from an otherwise anonymous figure known as 'the Friend of God from the Oberland'. Although scholars largely concur that these were in fact written by Merswin himself, they are reflective (often wildly so) of themes found in Eckhart and Tauler.

Generally, however, the teaching found in Merswin's writings is conventional and tame, even when it touches (lightly enough) on some of the familiar chords of the *via negativa*, as in this passage from *The Book of the Nine Rocks*:

> ... many unintelligent men will be amazed by it; but rational, godly men will understand that one must portray these things in images if men will comprehend it, for God is too great for man to conceive him. Tell me, you say you fear that some men may not understand it and think

incomprehensible all that I have had you write of the nine rocks. There are still men who will understand it, even though they be few.[17]

The absence of depth and brilliance in Merswin's teaching presaged the decline of Rhineland mysticism, for his successor, Nicholas of Basle, seems to have veered ever further toward the edge of orthodoxy. In 1409, he was tried and executed for heresy at Vienna. With his death, the Friends of God disappear as a historical movement, although their influence survived, surprisingly enough, among the mystical Anabaptists and through them, the Mennonites, Hutterites, Amish, and English Baptist tradition.

The Book of Spiritual Poverty

Composed by an unknown writer sometime in the latter half of the fourteenth century, *The Book of Spiritual Poverty* (*Das Buch von geistlicher Armuth*) focuses on the Rhineland theme of evangelical poverty as a source of detachment, of liberty, and purity of action, which makes the soul a 'friend of God'. Attributed to Tauler for many years, this little work is a compendium of Rhineland motifs, but already contains elements of the *devotio moderna*, with its emphasis on the imitation of Christ, 'mortification', the acquisition of virtue, and obtaining peace of heart by abandoning the world.[18]

The little *Book* was not without its critical admirers, however. In 1543 it was excerpted by St Peter Canisius, the first German Jesuit, in his *Holy Instructions of Tauler*. In 1548, the Carthusian Laurence Surius translated the whole book into Latin, also as a work of Tauler. As C. F. Kelley observes, 'His publication became so popular throughout Europe that French, Italian, Spanish and Dutch translations of all the treatises which bore Tauler's name were circulated', although not without serious consequences in the Counter-Reformation, as we have seen.[19]

Commenting on a passage from St Paul, 'He who is joined

to God becomes one spirit with God' (1 Cor. 6:17), the author explains,

> This joining is simply the spirit going out of herself, out of time, and entering into a pure *nothingness*. That which is and which forms her being is the divine likeness which dwells in man and which man can never destroy. God takes this likeness and unites it with Himself and in this way the spirit of man becomes one spirit with God according to the divine likeness.[20]

In Part III, addressing the theme of 'Sinking into the Godhead', he alludes repeatedly to Eckhart's teaching: 'The true lovers of God also love Him with all their mind, and this is when their mind rises above all created things and penetrates into the uncreated good, which is God Himself, and then loses itself in the secret darkness of the unknown God. It loses itself in Him and breaks through Him so that it cannot return.'[21] True to the teaching of Eckhart and Tauler, the author teaches with regard to the value of continually dying to self that

> by it God is born in the soul. In other words, when God transports the spirit from the soul and throws her into the darkness of His Godhead, he transforms her with His Godhead so that she becomes like God. She loses the shape of creatureliness, and is formed into the formless image of the Son in the Godhead; hence, the man becomes a son of grace in the way that he is a son of nature.[22]

Such observations could well have come from the pen of Tauler or even Eckhart. But the larger part of the book is replete with reflections of a much more conventional piety, outlining an ascetical rather than mystical path to union with God. Similarly, the *Theologia Germanica*, composed by a Teutonic knight of Sachsenhausen, near Frankfurt, around Eckhartian themes, falls conspicuously short of the teaching of the great German Dominicans.

The German Theology

Although lacking the brilliance of the Rhineland preachers, the *Theologia Germanica*, which had so great an influence on Luther, is a work of solid and orthodox spirituality.[23] In terms much like those found in Catherine of Siena, the author first savours the fullness of God through a consideration of human nothingness or radical spiritual poverty. Later, however, he introduces the theme of the nameless divinity, touches lightly on the no-thingness of God, and even the birth of God in the soul, without, however, mentioning the divine darkness.

> Christ has also said: 'No man comes to Me, except the Father, who has sent Me, draw him' [John 6:44]. Now mark: by the Father, I understand the Perfect, Simple Good, which is All and above All, and without which and besides which there is no true Substance, nor true Good, and without which no good work ever was or will be done. And in that it is All, it must be in All and above All. And it cannot be any one of those things which the creatures, as creatures, can comprehend or understand. For whatever the creature, as creature (that is, in her creaturely nature), can conceive of and understand, is something, a this or that, and therefore some sort of creature. And now if the Simple Perfect Good were somewhat, a this or that, which the creature understands, it would not be the All, nor the Only One, and therefore not Perfect. Therefore also it cannot be named, seeing that it is none of all the things which the creature as creature can comprehend, know, conceive, or name. Now behold, when this Perfect Good, which is unnamable, flows into a Person able to bring forth, and brings forth the Only-begotten Son in that Person, and itself in Him, we call it the Father.[24]

Such gingerly approaches to the soaring themes of Dionysian mysticism were heartily abandoned in favour of the emphatic language so characteristic of Eckhart when another writer of the late fourteenth century, an anonymous Englishman from the north-central Midlands, undertook the direction of a young would-be hermit.

The Cloud of Unknowing

In the work by which he is named, this elusive spiritual master, uniquely in the English tradition, erected an entire doctrine on a thoroughly Dionysian foundation. He also translated (and expanded) the *Mystical Theology* as *Deonise Hid Divinity*, and supplied his eager young disciple (also anonymous) with several more commentaries.[25]

While the author's emphasis on the helplessness of knowing and the unifying power of love reflects the approach of Thomas Gallus, with whose Dionysian commentaries he was familiar, many characteristic themes of Rhineland mysticism are also palpably present. The writings of the *Cloud* author are, seemingly, the only English works of the period which show this influence, which led Dom David Knowles to suspect a Dominican provenance (which is supported also by his allusions to Thomas Aquinas, whose teaching was by no means widely favoured outside of Dominican circles at this time).[26] One way or another, the themes of unknowing, the cloud of darkness, and the nothingness of God, as well as that of the searching soul, are nowhere more eloquently rendered.

In the third chapter we are told,

> ... at first ... you find but a darkness, and as it were a cloud of unknowing, you know not what, saving that you feel in your will a naked intent unto God. This darkness and this cloud, howsoever you do, is betwixt you and your God, and hinder you, so that you may neither see him clearly by light of understanding in your reason, nor feel him in sweetness of love in your affection. And therefore struggle to bide in this darkness as long as you may, evermore crying after him whom you love. For if ever you shall see him or feel him, as it may be here, it must always be in this cloud and in this darkness.[27]

In the sixth chapter, the author explains in terms even Aquinas would find acceptable, why it is 'longing love' that drives the mystical adventure forward through the obscurity of unknowing:

> ... of all other creatures and their works – yea, and of the works of God himself – may a man through grace have fulness of knowing, and well can he think of them; but of God himself can no man think. And therefore I would leave all that thing that I can think, and choose to my love that thing that I cannot think. For why, he may well be loved, but not thought. By love may he be gotten and holden; but by thought neither. And therefore, although it be good sometime to think on the kindness and the worthiness of God in special, and although it be a light and a part of contemplation, nevertheless in this work it shall be cast down and covered with a cloud of forgetting. And you shall step above it stalwartly, but joyfully, with a devout and a pleasing stirring of love, and try to pierce that darkness above you. And smite upon that thick cloud of unknowing with a sharp dart of longing love; and go not thence for aught that occurs.

As shown by Dom Justin McCann and others, although unique in its penchant for Dionysian, even Rhinish spiritual themes, the *Cloud* literature continued to exert some influence, especially in Benedictine and Carthusian monastic circles, for centuries to come. But the last great exponent of the mystical way of the Rhineland mystics came neither from England nor from the southern reaches of the long river linking the meadows of the Alps to the North Sea, but from the Low Countries, and sometimes rather irritably.

Ruysbroeck

The writings of Jan van Ruysbroeck (1293–1381) and his followers at their monastic retreat at Groenendael, 'the Green Valley', would greatly influence the *devotio moderna* in the fifteenth century. The 'new spirituality' favoured by Thomas à Kempis and others would become less optimistic and more other-worldly as the fourteenth century descended into the gloom of the Great Western Schism and recurrent episodes of plague and violence, and there are glimpses of this tendency in Ruysbroeck. But for the most part his spirituality is an exuberant restatement and, as he saw it, a needed correction, of the brash teachings of the Friends of God, including Eckhart himself, although his knowledge of the Meister's works was faulty.

Ruysbroeck's works, principally *The Spiritual Espousals*, the *Kingdom of the Lovers of God* and the *Seven Steps of the Ladder of Spiritual Love*, and other writings such as *The Seven Enclosures* and *A Mirror of Eternal Blessedness*, remain classics of western spirituality.[28] Much as had Eckhart and Tauler half a century earlier, Ruysbroeck attempted to chart the way into the incomprehensible and nameless heart of God. Ironically, the more he strives to distance himself from the excesses of Dionysian exuberance, the more he sounds like Eckhart. As a result, he too was later criticized by Jean Gerson, the chancellor of the University of Paris and a spiritual writer of note. Despite all this, Ruysbroeck's works were revered by his followers and have remained classical statements of the *via negativa*. In 1908, Ruysbroeck was beatified by Pope Pius X.

Ruysbroeck's debt to the classical tradition of Christian agnosticism (and both Beguine and Rhineland themes) is announced clearly in *The Spiritual Espousals*:

> The sublime nature of the Godhead will be seen and beheld as simplicity and unicity, inaccessible height and unfathomable depth, incomprehensible breadth and eternal length, a dark stillness and a wild desert, a repose for all the saints in unity and a bliss common to itself and all the saints for eternity. A person could also behold many a wonder in the fathomless sea of the Godhead. Although we make use of sensible images because of the coarseness of the senses with which we give external expression to

it, in truth it will be seen from within to be a fathomless good from which all particular forms or modes are excluded. But when we give external expression to it, then we attribute to it images and modes in many different ways, according to the degree of enlightenment of the particular human reason which brings it to expression.[29]

Like Eckhart, Ruysbroeck teaches that, in the end, the seeking soul will encounter the empty desert of the Godhead, where all distinctions, and all names and concepts are enveloped in the divine darkness where even the divine Persons are lost in simple, ineffable unity. But such union is also an embrace of joyful love in which creature and Creator lose all awareness of differentiation. Thus, 'in this darkness an incomprehensible light is born and shines forth; this is the Son of God, in whom a person becomes able to see and to contemplate eternal life.'[30]

On Learned Ignorance: Nicholas of Cusa

The last of the medieval spiritual writers to espouse the *via negativa* into his teaching was the German cardinal, statesman, mathematician, and philosopher, Nicolas of Cusa (1400–64), who belongs perhaps more to the world of the Renaissance than to the Middle Ages.[31] Although his insight into the 'dark' or negative knowledge of God occurred to him independently of the Rhineland tradition, he later studied, among other works of medieval mysticism, Eckhart's Latin writings, annotated copies of which are found in the learned cardinal's immense library. And though consciously indebted to the classical Christian tradition of Dionysian mysticism, Nicholas also developed startlingly original interpretations that soon developed into a major theological controversy.

In a perceptive appraisal of Nicholas and his sources, Donald Duclow points out that,

> Albert the Great and Eckhart accord intellect a central place in their spirituality. Nicholas's annotated manu-

scripts of [Eriugena's] *Periphyseon*, Albert's Dionysian commentaries and Eckhart's Latin works thus provide important evidence of his sources on these issues. Other figures in the Albertist school also influenced Cusanus. As a young man he studied at the University of Cologne which was heir to Albert's Dominican studium, and there he became a close friend of Heimeric de Campo. Through Heimeric Nicholas came to know the earlier Dominican thinkers Dietrich of Freiburg, Ulrich of Strassburg and Berthold of Moosburg – all of whom developed Albert's teachings on intellect.[32]

Already by the end of the fourteenth century, however, the way of unknowing was rapidly diminishing as a dominant feature of Rhineland spirituality, at least in its more vigorous Dionysian expression. After the suppression of the Beguines, beginning in 1311, it soon disappeared from French and Flemish spirituality as well. Its presence in *The Cloud of Unknowing*, Jan van Ruysbroeck, and Nicholas of Cusa tends to be exceptional rather than typical, the *dernier cri* of a tradition that in the collapse of scholasticism and the disintegration of medieval Christendom itself, had run its course.

8. IN THE END, GOD

In the same manner shalt thou do with this little word GOD. Fill thy spirit with the ghostly meaning of it . . . and mean God wholly, and wholly God, so that nought work in thy mind and in thy will, but only God.

The Cloud of Unknowing, Chapter 40

Some form of faithful agnosticism seems to be ingredient in all religious traditions. Because of its roots in the biblical tradition and the metaphysical ruminations of the late classical era, Negative Theology is clearly part of the spiritual and theological inheritance of Christianity, perhaps irrepressibly so. It flares out in expected ways, whether in Barthian Neo-Orthodoxy, with its emphasis on the 'wholly otherness' of God, or even in the 'God is Dead' enthusiasms of Schubert Ogden and other 'Christian atheists' in the halcyon 1960s. The end-of-the-century revival of interest in early Greek and Latin Christianity as well as medieval spirituality has also reawakened a generation of younger scholars to the heuristic potential of Ways of Unknowing.

The insistence of Lorenzo Valla, Erasmus, and the Lutheran scholars of the Renaissance that the Dionysian writings could not have been sub-apostolic undoubtedly played some role in the eclipse of apophatic mysticism, especially during the Platonic revival of the sixteenth century in philosophy and the arts.[1] The 'Dark Knowledge of God' would resurface, briefly, in the writings of Denis the Carthusian, his confrère, Laurence Surius, and St John of the Cross, as well as in more explicitly Thomistic commentaries of John of St Thomas. More destructively, it appears in the iconoclasm of the Roundheads and the Huguenots. But the spiritual agenda of Reformation and Counter-Reformation preachers and writers differed considerably from that of the late Middle Ages. The *via negativa* of Albert, Thomas, and Eckhart was not the road taken by Martin Luther, John Calvin, Ignatius of Loyola, Teresa of Ávila, Francis de Sales, nor even George Fox. With the exceptions noted, the ancient way of unknowing was regarded, if it was considered at all, as either a detour or a cul-de-sac.

But if the way of the Rhineland mystics faded from prominence in the fifteenth and sixteenth centuries, the prophetic inheritance of Catherine of Siena and her disciples produced successes of a wholly different magnitude.

CATHERINE'S LEGACY

The movement towards reform and renewal within the Order began in Germany and the Netherlands. Stimulated in Italy by Catherine's activities and writings, the cause of more strict observance was championed by members of her 'family', Raymond of Capua, Bartholomew of Siena, Thomas Caffarini, and John Dominici. The election of Raymond as Master of the Order in 1380 would have repercussion for several centuries, especially in Italy and Spain, where the tension between Observants and Conventuals more than once threatened to shatter the unity of the Order. According to Ashley,

> On the whole Raymond's method succeeded, but it was based on the assumption which today must be questioned that religious renewal can be a literal return to 'primitive observance' in the face of historical changes. He failed to distinguish between those elements of Dominican life which define its permanent purpose and those which had become obsolete.[2]

Despite the lingering problems introduced by Raymond's single-minded devotion to reform, unexpected benefits also arose, not least as a result of his appointment of Bl. John

Dominici, another of Catherine's disciples, as vicar of the reform in Italy. For through his efforts toward the renewal of the Order, like those of his confrère, St Antoninus of Florence, there arose an openness to the arts that would shortly blossom into the magnificent achievements of Bl. John of Fiesole, baptized as Guido di Piero, but known to the whole world as Fra Angelico.[3]

THE ANGEL OF JUDGEMENT

The prophetic spirit associated with Catherine was by no means limited to Italy. Paramount among preachers of the late Middle Ages was St Vincent Ferrer (1350–1419), the apocalyptic miracle-worker of Spain and France.[4]

Like many religious enthusiasts of the period, Vincent was wary of the metaphysical flights of the Rhineland tradition, and was, like his contemporary, Thomas à Kempis, unfavourably inclined toward intellectual approaches to religion in general. He was an astounding preacher and undeniably saintly. Yet he also picked the wrong papal contender in the Great Western Schism and was just as mistaken about the End of the World, which he predicted to be imminent and supported by a number of miracles.

As a spiritual writer, Vincent occasionally evinces originality and psychological insight. In a passage such as this, he comes close to Teresa of Ávila:

> Let your whole concern, then, be to possess your soul in peace and serenity of heart. Do not be cast down by anything that happens, except your own sins and those of others and anything that might further be an occasion of sin to you. Let no accident trouble or disquiet you. Do not allow yourself to become angry at the faults of others. Cherish sentiments of sympathy and compassion for all, recognizing that you yourself would be much worse than they, did not Christ Jesus preserve you by his grace.[5]

Generally, however, even at his best, Vincent is more a moral-

izer than a mystagogue.[6] That the spiritual climate had chilled
considerably in the wake of the Black Death and the Great
Western Schism is evident in the following passage in which
he tries to maintain the tradition of spiritual discipleship, but
capitulates to the realities of the day:

> Unfortunately, it must be admitted, that nowadays
> scarcely anyone is to be found capable of directing others
> in the way of perfection. Nay more, a person who wishes
> to tend toward God will find many who will seek to dis-
> suade him and hardly a single one who will agree to help
> him.
>
> We must therefore have recourse to God with all our
> heart, praying Him earnestly and humbly to teach us
> Himself and casting ourselves into His arms with complete
> abandonment to His divine Providence. Touched by our
> confidence, He will receive us kindly as poor orphans; for
> He wills not the death of anyone, but that all should arrive
> at the knowledge of truth.[7]

The prophetic element in Dominican preaching certainly did
not die out with the fiery preacher from Valencia, however.
The final flourishing of the Dominican reform movement produced the great Italian preacher, prophet, and political
reformer, Girolamo Savonarola, who in 1498 met a martyr's
death with two members of his community at St Mark's in
Florence.

THE MEDDLESOME FRIAR

Born in 1452, Savonarola entered the Dominicans at Bologna
in 1474.[8] There he befriended the young Giovanni Pico della
Mirandola, one of the most brilliant of the early Renaissance
humanists. An adherent of the ancient *via negativa*, for Pico,
as he wrote in his book *De Ente et Uno*, God was clothed in
darkness, known only imperfectly by the human mind. Savonarola opposed him in this (and other matters), but being far
more broad-minded than commonly supposed, when Pico died

in 1494 at the age of thirty-one, Savonarola clothed him at his request in the Dominican habit.

Evangelically suspicious of the Platonizing tendencies of the intellectuals of Florence when he became Prior of San Marco in 1491, Savonarola nevertheless permitted them to meet in the priory and freely debated them. Far from being an iconoclast, he supported the arts and during one crisis, purchased the entire Medici library, using the priory itself as collateral, to prevent it from being carted off to France by the army of Charles VII.

The eloquent and fearless friar engaged in controversy on almost every front. He preached against decadence in art and morals, castigated civil corruption, and opposed corruption in the Church, particularly under the venomous leadership of Pope Alexander VI. Savonarola's stringent reforms ensured his downfall, however, which was engineered by a cabal of papal agents and Florentine political mobsters. Arrested on trumped-up charges of sedition, the aging friar was subjected to weeks of horrendous torture. After a forced confession, which he later retracted, Savonarola and two of his closest Dominican disciples were dragged to the public square on 25 May 1498, where they were hanged and their bodies burned.

Many Florentines venerated Savonarola as a saint and martyr, and, in later years, his canonization was urged by St Philip Neri and St Catherine de' Ricci, who was cured of a serious illness through his intercession. Recently, Savonarola's cause was reintroduced.

In addition to his extant poems and sermons, fifteen of which were placed on the Index of Forbidden Books, Savonarola's works include his *Compendium of Revelations* (1495), *The Triumph of the Cross* (1497), and *The Simplicity of the Christian Life*. Themes of detachment, poverty, and love found in Eckhart and Catherine are also found here. Guy Bedouelle cites a short sermon in which the following excerpt can be taken as indicative:

'Behold, let us show you the crucified Christ: he is our

true love. O, how this Crucified One is Love itself!' He is indeed. And so I grasped him, and I said, 'Are you love?' He responded, *'I am the man who has seen poverty.'* O, why are you poor? 'Because love is always poor: love forgets everything else, except for the thing beloved. I was very rich, and now I have become poor; I used to have everything, and now I seem to have nothing. And so I would wish that you could forget everything, and I would want to make you love with me, and we would be one love together.'[9]

A NEW ERA

During the next several centuries Dominican spirituality would develop in manifold directions, generally along lines followed by European Christianity as a whole. As devotion and 'piety' replaced the robust mystical and prophetic spirit of the Middle Ages, an almost obsessional cultivation of virtue and the defence of orthodox Roman Catholicism loomed ever larger in the spiritual as well as the theological agenda. The Order of Preachers was no exception to this trend. In particular, because of its close association with Dominican friars in Spain, the shadow of the Inquisition would darken the image of the Order in both Protestant and Catholic lands for centuries to come, although Dominicans had no monopoly on the role of Inquisitor.

In the years to come, outstanding representatives of the Order would achieve distinction and sanctity in many fields, whose extent and depth prevent anything more than a cursory glance here. In Spain, the lectures and writings of Francisco de Vitoria (*c.* 1483–1546) prepared the foundation for the work of Bartolomé de las Casas, the tireless defender of Native Americans in the following century. In Peru, the Dominican Order produced the first canonized saint of the New World, Rose of Lima, and two friar contemporaries, St Martin de Porres, the most popular saint in Latin America today, and St Juan Maçias, both lay brothers.[10]

In the Old World, the Italian reform movement which culmi-
nated in the death of Savonarola produced its latest if fairest
fruit in the life and letters of the mystic, St Catherine de' Ricci,
so like her namesake, Catherine of Siena. Her devotion to the
memory of Savonarola became a temporary obstacle to her
canonization but resulted in a reconsideration of the preacher's
sanctity, which may eventuate in his own canonization.[11]

Many other Dominican saints, mystics, and spiritual writers
contributed valuably to the Order, the Church, and the world
in the following centuries. Their lives have been told elsewhere, however, and even a cursory glance would take us far
beyond the limits of the present work.[12] Here, however, we
may well ask especially with respect to the ways of unknowing
so central to the concerns of Thomas, Eckhart, and the Rhineland Dominican tradition in particular, what relevance any of
it might have for women and men today?

THE LITTLE WORD 'GOD'[13]

At the tender age of five, according to his biographers, Thomas
Aquinas startled and dismayed his teachers by asking
(repeatedly) 'What is God?' At the end of his life he no longer
asked, because he knew that no one *can* know what God is.
Knowing *that* God exists, and *must* exist, is far different from
knowing even what we mean when we say 'God'. Today,
however, we seem more comfortable with what 'God' means
(or doesn't) than whether God exists (or doesn't).

At the beginning of *A History of God*, Karen Armstrong
recites the catechism answer to the question 'What is God?',
one she seems to have accepted despite misgivings until well
into her adult life: 'God is the supreme spirit, Who alone exists
of Himself and is infinite in all perfections.'[14] She now considers
that wrong as well as politically incorrect. At the end of what is
actually a long and interesting exploration of human religions,
Armstrong nevertheless affirms that the world needs a 'work-
able' notion of God, if only to prevent our destroying ourselves.
Presumably, as has been the case for 14,000 years, humans

will develop a suitable model. Probably several, as Sallie McFague and other theologians have suggested.[15]

Similarly, in *God: A Biography*, Jack Miles catalogues how the biblical portrayal of God developed over the course of Hebrew history as human behaviour changed, human thinking improved, and history itself acquired a discernible trajectory.[16] With compelling rigour, Miles shows how God's transcendence, particularly in the form of remoteness or obscurity, increases in the latter books of the Hebrew tradition, inexorably replacing the intimacy, awe, and occasional terror that marked divine visitations in earlier writings.

Ideas about God have undeniably changed a great deal over the centuries and they will no doubt continue to change. So much may be freely granted. The very proliferation of God-concepts argues strongly for their relativity as well as their inadequacy.[17] But what is left after we admit all the above? A receding deity whose main role in human experience is to keep us from committing collective suicide?

Perhaps not. In the last few years, several leading physicists and astronomers have expressed a new openness to reconsidering the existence of God as the field of creative possibility undergirding the fabric of the universe, a notion which would no doubt interest Thomas Aquinas (if not the late Carl Sagan). But, as Karen Armstrong complains, such concepts lack the sense of intimacy and care that for so long sustained the faith of Jews, Christians, and Muslims among other peoples of the world. We require something a little warmer and closer to home. The question most people seem to bring with them for spiritual counsel is what has God to do with *me* – with my life, my hopes, fears, and future?

Beyond God

The little word 'god' comes to us in English and related languages from an Indo-Germanic root which means 'to call upon someone'. A 'god' is one who is invoked. 'God' is thus not a name, but a title; behind the title is the Nameless One, whose

Name is not lacking, but beyond all naming. And at the heart
of the little word 'God' is a cry for help. Radically, to utter the
little word 'God' is to *pray*, to acknowledge our dependence
and reliance on a power and a presence totally beyond us and
unutterably near us. (One of the few English cognates of 'pray',
which comes from the Latin *precor*, is, not surprisingly,
'precarious'.) 'God' is the cry of a creature who recognizes if
not her creator, at least her createdness. Further, *only* a creature can cry 'God!'

It is to this fundamental meaning that Meister Eckhart
appeals in his amazing and notorious Sermon 52, leading us
not into light of vision, but into the darkness of faith. What
he and almost all the great mystics teach us is ultimately
disconcerting. For what they tell us is that the sovereign
experience of God's presence occurs in obscurity, absence, and
unfulfilled yearning, much as the biblical witness of the
ancient Jews ends in a perplexingly vanishing deity, the vision
of a vacant throne.

In preaching on spiritual poverty, Eckhart said,

> While I yet stood in my first cause, I had no God and was
> my own cause: then I wanted nothing and desired nothing,
> for I was bare being and the knower of myself in the
> enjoyment of truth. Then I wanted myself and wanted no
> other thing: what I wanted I was and what I was I wanted,
> and thus I was free of God and all things. But when I
> left my free will behind and received my created being,
> then I had a God. For before there were creatures, God
> was not God: He was That which He was. But when crea-
> tures came into existence and received their created being,
> then God was not God in Himself – He was God in
> creatures.[18]

To understand oneself as a creature means to find oneself
mysteriously apart from that Source of being, consciousness,
and bliss, yet yearning for closeness to it:

When I flowed forth from God, all creatures declared:

'There is a God'; but this cannot make me blessed, for
with this I acknowledge myself as a creature. But in my
breaking-through, where I stand free of my own will, of
God's will, of all His works, and of God himself, then I am
above all creatures and am neither God nor creature, but
I am that which I was and shall remain for evermore.[19]

For Eckhart, beatitude, true loving union with the Source of all
meaning and value, transcends all awareness of the difference
between Creator and creature. Thus, he can say, and say
rightly, 'I pray to God to make me free of God. . . .'[20]

If the ancient theologians and mystics are correct, when
we think we know what God is, we are furthest away from
understanding. Thomas Aquinas was right, and is indeed only
one voice in a vast chorus of mystical agnosticism. As Eckhart,
Catherine, the *Cloud* author, and Ruysbroeck profess, it is
when we open both our minds and hearts to the Incomprehensible that we grow closer to God. Then, liberated from the
shifting currents of politically correct divinities, constricting
images of hopes and needs projected onto the cosmos, and the
idols of the mind, we have a chance of recognizing the God in
the luminous darkness that remains. In Jürgen Moltmann's
words,

As Eckhart makes plain, the road from contemplation to
the mystical moment leads to the abolition of man's like-
ness to God for God's sake, and ultimately to the abolition
of God for God's sake. Then the soul is at home, then love
has found bliss, then passion ends in infinite enjoyment,
then the ineffable deification begins which the patristic
church called *theosis*.[21]

The consequences of such a logic of divine paradox are clear.
Whether in prayer, in thinking about God, in mediation, even
in art, fixity of shape must never go unchallenged. By itself,
the *via negativa* leads only into darkness and emptiness. But
as a corrective, the practice of 'unknowing', of 'ridding ourselves of God for the sake of God', emptying ourselves of God-

images (and self-images), allows for the process of continual and positive reformation by which alone we are gradually drawn toward the loving Presence of that God whose Name remains nameless.

NOTES

INTRODUCTION: A RECONCILIATION OF OPPOSITES

1. Several recent works in English have explored the spirituality of epochs and individuals, among them those by Gutiérrez, McGinn, Noffke, O'Driscoll, Tobin, Torrell, Tugwell, and Vicaire (see the bibliography for these and other references). Benedict Ashley's *The Dominicans* (Collegeville, MN: Liturgical Press, 1990) provides a useful if necessarily skeletal summary of Dominican spirituality as a whole. Similarly, William Hinnebusch's pre-Vatican II volume, *Dominican Spirituality: Principles and Practices* (Washington, DC: The Thomist Press, 1965) still contains many valuable insights, as does the even earlier volume of essays by French Dominicans edited by Anselm Townsend, *Dominican Spirituality* (Milwaukee: Bruce Publishing Co., 1934). But for reasons that should become abundantly evident in the following pages, a truly inclusive spiritual history of the Order of Preachers remains an elusive quarry, and perhaps always will.

2. Josef Pieper introduces his insightful discussion of the *via negativa* of St Thomas with this quotation from the Taoist, Lao-Tse: 'That name which can be pronounced / Is not the Eternal Name' (*The Silence of St Thomas*, tr. John Murray SJ and Daniel O'Connor (Chicago: Henry Regnery, 1965), p. 50).

3. William Stringfellow, *The Politics of Spirituality* (Philadelphia: Westminster Press, 1984), p. 22.

4. Kenneth Leech, *Soul Friend* (New York: Harper and Row, 1980), p. 34. Compare this older definition by the Dominican, Reginald Garrigou-Lagrange: 'The interior life is lived in the depths of the soul; it is the life of the whole [person], not merely one or other of his [or her] faculties' (*The Three Ways of the Spiritual Life* (Rockford, IL: TAN Books, 1977), p. 1).

5. Kevin W. Irwin, *Liturgy, Prayer and Spirituality* (New York: Paulist Press, 1984), p. 13. In a more scholarly vein, Dr Sandra Schneiders writes, similarly, 'Christian Spirituality is that particular actualization of the capacity for self-transcendence that is constituted by the substantial gift of the Holy Spirit establishing a life-giving relation-

ship with God in Christ within the believing community. It is thus trinitarian, christological, and ecclesial religious experience' (Sandra Schneiders IHM, 'Theology and Spirituality: Strangers, Rivals or Partners?' in *Horizons*, 13, 2 (1986): 266).

6. Simon Tugwell OP, *Ways of Imperfection* (Springfield, IL: Templegate, 1985), pp. vii-viii.

7. Joann Wolski Conn, *Spirituality and Personal Maturity* (New York: Paulist Press, 1989), p. 21.

8. J.A.T. Robinson, *The Body: A Study in Pauline Theology* (Philadelphia: Westminster Press, 1952), p. 19.

Chapter 1: THE DOMINICAN ORDER AND ITS SPIRITUAL TRADITION

1. Here, I differ from the late Anselm Townsend, who wrote, ' . . . While the religious life is essentially one, consisting, as it does, in the service of God by the perfection of charity, each religious Order and Congregation is differentiated from every other by its immediate aims and the means which it employs to those aims. Because of the difference of means there arise diverse spiritualities, that is to say, diverse ascetical and spiritual theories and practices which determine the ethos of the religious family. Hence, there is a Dominican spirituality, based upon the ascetical teaching of Saint Thomas, just as there is a Jesuit spirituality based upon the *Spiritual Exercises*, or a Carmelite spirituality whose origin is to be sought in Saint Theresa and Saint John of the Cross, and so forth' (Townsend 1934, preface, p. vii). Dominican spirituality is based on much more than the ascetical teaching of St Thomas, or even his doctrine as a whole. It flows from the entire life of the Order in all its members and has been articulated in varying ways by a number of gifted teachers, not all of whom look immediately to St Thomas for inspiration.

2. Cited in Ashley 1990, 16.

3. Bede Jarrett, *The English Dominicans* (London: Burns, Oates and Washbourne, 1937), p. 18.

4. Hinnebusch 1965, 44.

5. Ibid.

6. Lester K. Little, *Religious Poverty and the Profit Economy in the Middle Ages* (Ithaca: Cornell University Press, 1978), p. 166.

7. Ibid., 2. Hinnebusch adds, 'The contemplative aspect of the Order's life is found especially in elements borrowed from the monks and canons' (see *Summa Theologiae*, II-II, Question 188, Article 8, reply to objection 2. Hereafter, I will use the standard abbreviation *ST*, followed by Roman numerals for the various Parts, Q for 'Question' and 'A' for Article, and the preposition 'ad' for replies to various Objections.). The Constitutions enumerate three contemplative features of traditional monasticism among the four fundamental means

of attaining the Order's ends, namely, ' ... the three solemn vows of obedience, chastity and poverty, the regular life with its monastic observances, the solemn chanting of the Divine Office, and the assiduous study of sacred truth.' These are essential means which can never be radically altered. They separate the Dominican from the world, direct him to God, and oblige him to live a contemplative and penitential life in the pursuit of Christian perfection' (ibid., 3).

8. Ashley 1990, 20.

9. Ashley 1990, 21. He adds, 'Closely connected with prayer, so closely that I believe it should not be numbered as a distinct element, is the life of penance which is so prominent in Dominic's life. ... [C]ommon to all religions that emphasize contemplation, is the conviction that our love of pleasure and comfort must be tamed if real serenity of mind is to be achieved. Second is the Christian conviction that original and actual sin are facts of the human condition' (Ashley 1990, 22).

10. Ashley comments, 'Some have said that Dominic copied the poverty of St Francis, but ... Dominic's poverty had a different origin and motivation. He wanted to be poor to make his preaching credible to the poor who saw in the poverty of the Albigensian Perfect a holiness superior to that of the worldly Catholic clergy' (Ashley 1990, 23).

11. Hinnebusch 1965, 105. A generation earlier, M.-R. Cathala noted that 'it should be thoroughly understood that this indispensable study is, as it were, the foundation rigorously demanded by Dominican prayer. On the other hand, this latter is no less requisite, for it would involve a certain contradiction to speak of a theologian – or a preacher of God – who does not love' ('Dominican Prayer', in Townsend 1934, 108).

12. Ashley 1990, 24 (original in italics).

13. Commentary on the Gospel of John, Chap. 1, Lect. 8, No. 188.

14. The classic reference is the *ST*, II-II, Q. 188, A. 6: *Sicut enim maius est illuminare quam lucere solum, ita maius est contemplata aliis tradere quam solum contemplari.* ('For even as it is better to enlighten than merely to shine, so is it better to give to others what has been contemplated than merely to contemplate.')

15. See the still illuminating works of Yves Congar OP, *I Believe in the Holy Spirit* 3 vols. (London: Geoffrey Chapman/New York: Seabury, 1983), Ambrose Gardeil OP, *The Gifts of the Holy Ghost in Dominican Saints* (Milwaukee: Bruce, 1937), and A.-M. Henry OP, *The Holy Spirit* (New York: Hawthorn Books, 1960).

16. See *Meister Eckhart, Sermons and Treatises*, tr. M. O'C. Walshe, Vol. 3 (Longmead, Shaftesbury, Dorset: Element Books, 1987), pp. 11–60.

Chapter 2: DOMINIC AND THE EARLY PREACHERS

1. *Perfectae Caritatis*, no. 2, in Austin Flannery OP (ed. and tr.), *Vatican Council II: The Basic Sixteen Documents* (Northport, NY: Costello

Pub. Co., and rev. ed. Dublin: Dominican Publications, 1996), pp. 386–7.

2. For several centuries, it has been widely accepted that Dominic's father was a Guzmán. But, as R. F. Bennett wrote in 1937, 'It has become conventional to connect Dominic with the noble house of Guzmán; but scholars have never regarded the case made out by Brémond (*De Guzmana stirpe S. Dominici*, Romae 1740) as proven' (R. F. Bennett, *The Early Dominicans: Studies in Thirteenth-Century Dominican History*, Cambridge: The University Press, 1937, p. 20). Hinnebusch, on the other hand, accepts the identification of Dominic's parents with the houses of Guzmán and Aza (Hinnebusch 1966, I, 15–17). Simon Tugwell and Guy Bedouelle remain cautiously reticent.

3. In Hinnebusch's telling words, 'The family bred ecclesiastics and saints. Two brothers, Anthony and Mannes, became priests. Mannes and two nephews became Dominicans. Joan and Mannes have been beatified. Anthony, a man of great zeal and charity, is entitled venerable' (Hinnebusch 1966, I, 15). Dominic's brother's name is also spelled (more accurately) as Mames.

4. Little writes (p. 155), 'While the sources continue to be almost totally silent on Dominic, his activities came to be centered in an institution that did leave traces. In 1206, the missionaries established at Prouille, a tiny fortified locality close to Fanjeaux, west of Carcassonne and south-east of Toulouse, a religious house for females converted from Catharism. Bishop Fulk of Toulouse made the principal donation. In the spring of 1207 Berengar of Narbonne gave to Notre-Dame of Prouille the proprietary rights over a church at nearby Limoux. These were the first of several donations of property and privileges that would make of Prouille a religious house endowed in the old-fashioned way. Simon of Montfort, for example, after taking Carcassonne and settling at Fanjeaux, became a generous benefactor of Notre-Dame of Prouille. This community became an adjunct to the preaching mission after the manner of Catharist way-stations, run usually by women, where *perfecti* would retire to restore their health or merely to rest from the rigours of itinerant preaching and to prepare for the next round. Though the Catholic missionaries continued to beg for food, at Prouille they had guaranteed to them a certain measure of security.'

5. The estimate of Henry B. Lea, the influential historian of the Inquisition and no friend of the Catholic Church, that Dominic's influence on the course of the Crusade was 'historically imperceptible' is significant in this regard. See Bennett 1937, 21, note 2.

6. The growth of the Order of Preachers over the next several years has been richly chronicled in the standard lives of Dominic and the history of the early Dominicans. Among them, the monumental study by M.-H. Vicaire is fundamental. Other works by Tugwell, Bedouelle,

Hinnebusch, Little, Bennett, and Jarrett, among many others, provide various perspectives and valuable insights.

7. Most of the earliest accounts of Dominic's life, sanctity, and miracles can be found in *Early Dominicans. Selected Writings*, edited with an introduction by Simon Tugwell OP (New York: Paulist Press, 1982). See also Vladimir Koudelka OP, *Dominic*, ed. and tr. Simon Tugwell (London: Darton, Longman and Todd, 1997).

8. Cited by Hyacinth Petitot OP, 'Saint Dominic – His Physical And Moral Physiognomy', in Townsend 1934, 1.

9. Simon Tugwell OP, *Saint Dominic* (Strasbourg: Éditions du Signe, 1995), 47.

10. Although extreme by today's standards, Dominic's physical practices were not unusual in the thirteenth century and were especially favoured among the Cathars, who instantly recognized in Dominic the comportment of a 'good man' (*un bonhomme*), whether friend or rival. His more typical and positive expressions of prayer are charmingly related in the very early text, 'The Nine Ways of Prayer of St Dominic', Tugwell 1982, 94–103. A beautifully illustrated facsimile of the medieval text is available through Dominican Publications, Dublin, Ireland (1996).

11. Tugwell 1982, 79.

12. Tugwell 1982, 25.

13. '. . . it was Dominic himself who initiated the policy of looking for recruits especially in University circles, and the emphasis on study in the Constitutions goes back at least to 1220, if not to 1216 (*Prim. Const.* I, 13: the novices are to be told that they ought to be "intent on study, always reading something or thinking about something, by day and by night, at home and abroad"; II 29 specifies that students can stay up at night, if they want to, to study). Ideally, in fact, study and prayer merged to form a whole life of attentiveness to God and his words and works (cf. William of Tocco, *Life of St Thomas Aquinas* 30.)' (Tugwell, 1982, 107, n. 27).

14. Raymond Martin OP, 'The Historical Development of Dominican Spirituality', Townsend 1934, 39–40.

15. Tugwell 1982, 'Introduction', 3–4.

16. For a synoptic presentation of Humbert's career as a Dominican and a selection of his writings, see Tugwell 1988, 31–4.

17. Martin, in Townsend 1934, 41.

18. Translated by Benedict Ashley, in Ashley 1990, 42–3.

19. Hinnebusch 1973, 288–9.

20. Resources on the life and teaching of St Albert include Tugwell 1988, and (in English) Sr Mary Albert OP, *Albert the Great* (River Forest, IL: *Spirituality Today* Supplement, Autumn, 1987 (revised ed. of *Albert the Great*, Oxford: Blackwell Publications, 1948)); James Weisheipl OP (ed.), *Albertus Magnus and the Sciences, Commemorative Essays* (Toronto: Pontifical Institute of Medieval Studies, 1980); H.

Wilms OP, *Albert the Great* (London: Burns, Oates and Washbourne, 1933); and Francis A. Catania, 'Albert the Great', *Encyclopedia of Philosophy* (New York: Macmillan and The Free Press, 1967), I, pp. 64–6.

21. Included in Simon Tugwell's edition of the selected writings of Albert and Thomas, 1988.

22. Cited in Hinnebusch 1965, 115.

23. Hinnebusch 1973, 298.

24. Tugwell 1988, 138–9. The reference is to Eph. 3:15.

25. Ibid., 153.

26. Hinnebusch 1973, 299. For Albert's view of our knowledge of God, see Tugwell 1988, 40–95, 134–98.

27. Other outstanding spiritual writers of the period include not only Albert's own students, but students of his students, including Eckhart the Younger, John Franko, Henry of Egwint, Giselher of Statheim, Henry de Calstris, Venturino of Bergamo, and Dalmatius Monerio.

28. Hinnebusch 1973, 300.

Chapter 3: THE DARKNESS OF GOD AND THE NEGATIVE WAY

1. Recent studies include the excellent volumes by Michael Sells, *Mystical Languages of Unsaying* (Chicago: University of Chicago Press, 1994), and Denys Turner, *The Darkness of God: Negativity in Christian Mysticism* (Cambridge: Cambridge University Press, 1995). The earlier brief volume by Charles Journet, *The Dark Knowledge of God* (London: Sheed and Ward, 1948), remains a valuable compendium of classical, largely Thomistic sources. Turner and Sells situate kataphatic and apophatic theologies in a dynamic dialectical system which ultimately subverts and destabilizes or at least relativizes all theological discourse.

2. *Oxford English Dictionary*, 389b. In an innovative move, Michael Sells indicates negative or apophatic theology by the term 'unsaying', drawing attention to the hidden or subversive function of such language. As *agnosia* ('unknowing') points by indirection to that which remains known to be unknown, so also *apophasis* or 'unsaying' can refer obliquely to what is left 'unsaid'. Linguistically, however, the parallel is imperfect, as the privative alpha of *a-gnosis* is not semantically equivalent to the prefix *apó-* ('away from', 'from', or 'off').

3. Unlike *apophasis, kataphasis* has no grammatical, rhetorical, or other equivalent in English usage. But both *kataphasis* and *apophasis* were part of the ordinary legal and philosophical vocabulary of ancient Greece, and seem not to have acquired a more technical sense, especially in theology, until the beginning of the Common Era. Both terms have multiple and parallel lexical connections and therefore manifest semantic ambiguity. Just as *kataphasis* can be formed from three Greek verbs, *kataphainō* (declare, make public), *kataphaskō*

(answer, affirm), and *kataphēmi* (assent), so also *apophasis* arises from either *apophainō* (show or declare), *apophaskō* (deny), or *apophēmi* (speak out, declare). Thus, even *apophasis* can mean 'decree', 'judgement', or 'declaration', as well as 'negation' and 'denial'. Insisting on a narrow, rigid, and exclusive understanding of these terms is characteristic of modern rather than classical approaches to language and reality.

4. Some English-speaking authors including Andrew Louth and Denys Turner have adopted the convention of referring to the 'Pseudo-Areopagite' as 'Denys', one of the spellings of the name, along with 'Deonise' and 'Denis', used by the fourteenth-century author of *The Cloud of Unknowing*. Although 'Dionysios' would be more accurate and, to my way of thinking, more appropriate, in this book I have observed ordinary Latinate tradition and call him simply 'Dionysius' or 'the Areopagite' without qualifying either element as 'Pseudo'.

5. The classic references are to *The Mystical Theology*, and a number of passages in *The Divine Names*. See *Pseudo-Dionysius: The Complete Works*, tr. Colm Luibheid, foreword, notes and collaboration by Paul Rorem, preface by René Roques, and intro. by Jaroslav Pelikan, Jean Leclercq, and Karlfried Froelich (New York: Paulist Press, 1987).

6. See Deut. 4:11, 'And you came near and stood at the foot of the mountain, while the mountain burned with fire to the heart of heaven, wrapped in darkness [*choshek*], cloud [*'anan*], and gloom [*'araphel*].' Other typical references include Deut. 5:23, 2 Sam. 22:10–12, 1 Kings 8:12, Ps. 18:9–11, Ps. 97:2, etc.

7. Ambiguous references also occur in Ps. 88:12–14, 18; Ps. 139:11–12, and elsewhere.

8. Samuel Terrien has explored this theme more thoroughly than any biblical writer I am aware of in his superb book, *The Elusive Presence* (San Francisco: Harper and Row, 1978). *Cathar* is not the only word used to convey God's hiddenness, even in Isaiah. See Isa. 1:15, 'When you spread forth your hands, I will veil [*'alam*] my eyes from you; even though you make many prayers, I will not listen; your hands are full of blood' and 30:20, 'And though the Lord give you the bread of adversity and the water of affliction, yet your Teacher will not withdraw [*kanaph*] himself any more, but your eyes shall see your Teacher.' For some reason, the word *chaba'*, with roughly the same meaning, seems never to be used of God: see Gen. 3:8 and 10, etc.

9. *First Apology*, Chap. 6. Cited in J. Quasten, *Florilegium Patristicum*, 14–16.

10. *Stromata* V, 2 (PG 9, 109a), cited by Lossky (1957), p. 34.

11. See the important essay by Louis Bouyer, 'Mysticism, An Essay on the History of the Word', in *Understanding Mysticism*, ed. Richard Woods OP (Garden City, NY: Image, 1980), pp. 42–55.

12. For an incisive exploration of this determining moment in spiritual history, see Andrew Louth, *The Origins of the Christian Mystical*

Tradition (Oxford: Clarendon Press, 1981), 52–97, and Rowan Williams, *The Wound of Knowledge* (London: Darton, Longman and Todd, 1990), 52–4.

13. For a brief but illuminating synopsis of the mystical theology of Gregory of Nyssa, see Louis Bouyer, *The Spirituality of the New Testament and the Fathers*, Vol. I of *A History of Christian Spirituality* (London: Burns and Oates, 1968), pp. 362–8.

14. *Oratio* 6, 'On the Beatitudes', PG 44, 1264–6.

15. Gregory of Nyssa, *The Life of Moses*, tr., intro., and notes by Everett Ferguson and Abraham J. Malherbe, preface by John Meyendorff (New York: Paulist Press, 1978), pp. 94–5.

16. Louth 1981, 95.

17. Louth 1981, 96. For Gregory of Nyssa on love, also see Bouyer 1968, 367–8.

18. From *Oratio* 38, 7 PG 36, 317B. Paraphrased in Lossky, p. 36.

19. *Enarrationes in Psalmos*, LXXXV, 12.

20. *Sermones de Scripturi Novi Testamenti*, 50, 6: 16.

21. *De Trinitate*, VII, iv, 7. In a passage reminiscent of Ignatius of Antioch, Augustine affirms that 'God is not even to be called ineffable, because to say even this is to speak of Him. Thus there arises a curious conflict of words; for if the ineffable is that which cannot be spoken, it is not ineffable if it can be spoken of as ineffable. And this conflict of words is rather to be avoided by silence than to be reconciled by speech' (*De Doctrina Christiana*, I, 6, 6). For a critical analysis of this important text, see both Turner and Sells.

22. *Confessions*, Book X, vii. Cited by Louth, p. 142.

23. *De Trinitate*, XV, xvii, 31, cited by Louth, p. 158. Perhaps no writer of antiquity more eloquently elegized love and desire for God than in Augustine's justly famous and often quoted passage from the *Confessions*: 'Late have I loved Thee, O Beauty so ancient and so new; late have I loved Thee! For behold Thou wert within me, and I outside; and I sought Thee outside and in my perversity fell upon those lovely things that Thou has made. Thou wert with me and I was not with Thee. I was kept from Thee by those things, yet had they not been in Thee, they would not have been at all. Thou didst call and cry to me and break open my deafness: and Thou didst send forth Thy beams and shine upon me and chase away my blindness: Thou didst breathe fragrance upon me, and I drew in my breath and do now pant for Thee: I tasted Thee, and now hunger and thirst for Thee: Thou didst touch me, and I have burned for Thy peace' (Book X, 27, tr. F. J. Sheed, cited by Louth 1981, 167–8).

24. *Ninth Sermon on the Nativity*, PL LIV, c. 226.

25. Dionysius the Areopagite, *Letter 1 to Gaius*, PG III, c. 1065. Luibhead 1987, 263. This passage will be cited by St Thomas Aquinas, ST II-II, Q. 180, A. 5, ad 1.

26. *The Divine Names*, chap. 1. Luibhead, p. 49. For the theme of love

(divine eros) in Dionysius, see *The Divine Names*, Luibheid 1987, 81–2; Andrew Louth, *Denys the Areopagite* (London: Geoffrey Chapman/Wilton, CT: Morehouse-Barlow, 1989), 94–6, 102–6, and Williams 1981, 119–20.

27. For excellent synopses of the Dionysian doctrine, see the introductory matter in the Classics of Western Spirituality volume edited and translated by Luibheid and Rorem, the relevant chapters in Louth and Williams, and Simon Tugwell's fine summary in *Albert and Thomas: Selected Writings* (New York: Paulist Press, 1988), pp. 39–44.

28. *Instructions on Faith*, I, 3–5.

29. *De Fide Orthodoxa*, I, 4, (PG 94, 800B), cited by Lossky, p. 36.

30. *Periphyseon* (*De Divisione Naturae*), ed. I. P. Sheldon-Williams (Dublin: Institute for Advanced Studies, 1978), Vol. 1, p. 522.

31. For the apophatic mysticism of Plato, Philo, and Plotinus, see Louth 1981, chapters 1–3; for Plotinus and Ibn Arabi, see Sells 1994, chapters 1, 3, and 4; and, on similar themes in Hindu religion, see Bimal Krishna Matilal, 'Mysticism and Ineffability: Some Issues of Logic and Language', *Mysticism and Language*, ed. Steven T. Katz (New York and Oxford: Oxford University Press, 1992), 143–57.

32. For an account of this development, see Tugwell 1988, 54–5.

33. Bonaventure, *The Soul's Journey into God* and other works, tr. and intro. by Ewart Cousins, preface by Ignatius Brady OFM (New York: Paulist Press, 1978), 113–15. Bonaventure weaves into his narrative the allied theme of seeking the face of God and the death that must follow: 'But if you wish to know how these things come about, ask grace not instruction, desire not understanding, the groaning of prayer not diligent reading, the Spouse not the teacher, God not man, darkness not clarity, not light but the fire that totally inflames and carries us into God by ecstatic unctions and burning affections. This fire is God, and *his furnace is in Jerusalem* [Isa. 31:9]; and Christ enkindles it in the heat of his burning passion, which only he truly perceives who says: *My soul chooses hanging and my bones death* [Job 7:15]. Whoever loves this death can see God because it is true beyond doubt that man will not see me and live [Exod. 33:20]. Let us, then, die and enter into the darkness . . .' (Ibid., p. 116. Also see Turner, chapter 5.)

Chapter 4: KNOWING THE UNKNOWABLE GOD: THE THREEFOLD PATH OF THOMAS AQUINAS

1. Recent resources on the life, doctrine, and spirituality of St Thomas Aquinas include the now-classic biography by James A. Weisheipl OP, *Friar Thomas d'Aquino: His Life, Thought, and Works* (Washington, DC: The Catholic University of America Press, rev. ed., 1983). The first part of Fr Jean-Pierre Torrel's monumental two-volume work, *L'Initiation à Saint Thomas d'Aquin: Sa personne et son oeuvre* (Paris:

Editions Cerf, 1993), which updates and in many instances corrects
Weisheipl, has been published in an English translation by Robert
Royal: *Saint Thomas Aquinas, Volume* I: *The Person and His Work*
(Washington, DC: The Catholic University of American Press, 1996).
The second volume, which treats of Thomas' spirituality and spiritual
doctrine, is awaiting publication in English. To these must be added
Simon Tugwell's brilliant introduction to *Albert and Thomas: Selected
Writings* (New York: Paulist Press, 1988), which is arguably the finest
short work yet published on Thomas' spiritual doctrine. Chenu's pio-
neering text remains essential reading despite its age: M.-D. Chenu
OP, *Towards Understanding St Thomas*, tr. Albert Landry OP and
Dominic Hughes OP (Chicago: Henry Regnery, 1963). It was Chenu,
as Fr Torrell reminds us, who so clearly revealed 'the "spirituality"
in which Thomas was rooted and the contemplation he pursued, while
fervently trying to share them with others' (p. xix). Benedict Ashley's
focused selection of texts from the biblical commentaries add to the
materials compiled by Tugwell: *Thomas Aquinas: The Gifts of the
Spirit – Selected Spiritual Writings*, Benedict Ashley OP, ed. and intro.,
translations by Matthew Rzeczkowski OP (Hyde Park, NY: New City
Press, 1996). Finally, there is the reader-friendly volume on Thomas
as a spiritual theologian by Robert Barron, *Thomas Aquinas: Spiritual Master* (New York: Crossroad, 1996).

2. Torrell 1996, xxi.
3. Ibid.
4. Townsend 1934, 47.
5. 'He wrote commentaries on Job, Psalms 1–54, Isaiah, Jeremiah, Lam-
   entations, the Gospels of Matthew and John, and most of the Epistles
   of St Paul, along with the *Golden Chain* of comments by the Greek
   and Latin Fathers on the Four Gospels, and two brilliant sermons on
   the value and scope of the Bible. These commentaries were written
   at various times and some are only student *reportationes*' (Ashley
   1990, 37).
6. Cited by Hinnebusch 1965, 89.
7. Ibid., 89–90.
8. Hinnebusch 1973, 303–4.
9. Ibid., 304. See James A. Weisheipl, *Friar Thomas d'Aquino*, 1974 ed.,
   315–16, 322–3.
10. For Thomas' teaching on union with God as a function of love, and
    the consequent primacy of charity in this life, see the *ST* I–II, Q. 27,
    A. 2, ad 2, and II–II, Q. 27, A. 4.
11. The key section on knowing and speaking about God in the first part
    of the *Summa Theologiae* (questions 12 and 13) is a tightly condensed
    exposition and development of *The Divine Names*. See Brian Davies
    OP, *The Thought of Thomas Aquinas* (Oxford and New York: Clarendon
    Press, 1992), pp. 43, and esp. 59–79. One of St Thomas' major works
    is in fact a lengthy commentary on Dionysius' book. It is at least

suggestive of the anti-Dionysian opprobrium of the Neo-thomistic revival earlier this century that this important work has not been translated into English, nor has it received much critical attention from Thomistic scholars in general. Thomas also gives extensive attention to the problem in *De Potentia*, his *Commentary on Boethius' De Trinitate*, his three-volume *De Veritate*, and elsewhere. See *De Veritate*, Art. III; IV *Sententiae.*, 49, 2, 7, ad 4; *Quodlibetales.*, I, 1; *Commentary on 2 Cor.*, c. 12, lect. 1; *ST* II–II, Q. 175, A. 4; Q. 180, A. 5; and the *Commentary on John*, c. 1, lect. 11.

12. *De Trinitate*, VII, iv, 7.

13. *The Degrees of Knowledge*, cited in Journet 1948, 65, emphasis added.

14. *ST* I, Q 13, A. 1 ad 1. Brian Davies comments, 'We can speak of God and mean what we say, but we cannot comprehend the reality which makes our statements true. Words such as "good" and "wise" truly characterize God, but they "fail to represent adequately what he is"' (Davies 1992, 62).

15. *De Potentia*, 7, 5 and 14.

16. St Thomas Aquinas, *Faith, Reason and Theology, Questions I–IV of his Commentary on the De Trinitate of Boethius*, trans. with intro. and notes by Armand Maurer (Toronto: Pontifical Institute of Mediaeval Studies, 1987), Q. I, Article 2. Hereafter: *Boethius*. In his brilliant essay on Thomas' negative knowledge, Josef Pieper remarks of this passage, 'I know of no text book of Thomistic thought which contains the notion expressed by St Thomas in his commentary on the *De Trinitate* of Boethius; namely, that there are three degrees in our knowledge of God: the lowest, the knowledge of God as He is active in creation; the second, the recognition of God as mirrored in spiritual beings; the third and loftiest, the recognition of God as the Unknown, *tamquam ignotum*. Or consider this sentence from the *Quaestiones Disputatae*: "This is what is ultimate in the human knowledge of God: to know that we do not know God," *quod (homo) sciat se Deum nescire*' (Pieper 1967, 69).

17. In the classical tradition, the thirteen proper attributes of God are unity, simplicity, perfection, goodness, infinity, omnipresence (ubiquity), immutability, eternity, wisdom, love, justice, mercy, and providence. Some, but not all, of these are in fact negations of their opposites, such as unity, simplicity, infinity, and immutability. See Journet 1948, 60.

18. *De Potentia*, 5, emphasis added.

19. For a concise summary of Thomas' teaching, see Journet 1948, 6. For a fuller discussion, see Davies 1992, ch. 4.

20. *In Boethius*, Maurer ed., A. 2.

21. These discussions are found in *ST* II-II, QQ. 171–89. For a selection of important passages, see Tugwell 1988. Also see *Thomas Aquinas: The Gifts of the Spirit: Selected Spiritual Writings*, ed. and intro. by Benedict Ashley OP, trans. by Matthew Rzeczkowski OP (Hyde Park,

NY: New City Press, 1996), which includes supportive material largely taken from the scriptural commentaries.

22. Hinnebusch 1965, 70–1.

23. The more relevant passages are found in *ST* II-II, QQ. 180–2 and 188, a. 6–7.

24. *ST*, Q. 182, A. 1 ad 5. Compare the following from his treatise *On Charity*: 'There are some who have ascended to such a summit of charity that they even put aside divine contemplation, though they delight greatly in it, that they might serve God through the salvation of their neighbors; and this perfection appears in Paul (see Rom. 9:3 and Phil. 1:23). Such also is the perfection proper to prelates and preachers and whosoever works to bring about the salvation of others. Hence they are symbolized by the angels on the ladder of Jacob, ascending through contemplation, descending, however, through the solicitude they feel for the salvation of their neighbors' (*De caritate*, a. 11, ad 6. Cited by Hinnebusch 1965, 76–7.) See also *ST* II-II, Q. 182, A. 2, and *Expos. in Canticum cant.* ii.

25. See, for instance, Richard Woods OP, ' "I am the Son of God": Eckhart and Aquinas on the Incarnation', *Eckhart Review*, June 1992, pp. 27–46.

Chapter 5: MEISTER ECKHART'S WAYLESS WAY AND THE NOTHINGNESS OF GOD

1. Excellent English translations of Eckhart's German works can be found in Meister Eckhart, *Sermons and Treatises*, tr. M. O'C. Walshe, 3 vols. (Longmead, Shaftesbury, Dorset: Element Books, 1987). For a rich selection of both German and Latin writings with valuable commentary see Meister Eckhart, *The Essential Sermons, Commentaries, Treatises and Defense*, ed. Bernard McGinn and Edmund Colledge (New York: Paulist Press, 1981) and *Meister Eckhart: Teacher and Preacher*, ed. and tr. Bernard McGinn with Frank Tobin and Elvira Borgstädt, preface by Kenneth Northcott (New York: Paulist Press / London: SPCK, 1987). A number of works in English on Eckhart have been published in recent years, among them, Oliver Davies, *Meister Eckhart: Mystical Theologian* (London: SPCK, 1991), Robert K. Forman, *Meister Eckhart: Mystic as Theologian* (Rockport, Mass./ Shaftesbury, Dorset: Element Books, 1991), Dom Cyprian Smith OSB, *Meister Eckhart: The Way of Paradox* (London: Darton, Longman and Todd, 1988), Frank Tobin, *Eckhart, Language and Thought* (Scranton: University of Pennsylvania Press, 1987), and Richard Woods OP, *Eckhart's Way* (London: Darton, Longman and Todd, 1987 / Collegeville, MN: Liturgical Press, 1991).

2. See Loris Sturlese, 'Mysticism and Theology in Meister Eckhart's Theory of the Image', *Eckhart Review* (August 1992): 18–31.

3. For a critical discussion of the close correspondence between many of

Eckhart's characteristic themes and those of the Beguines, see Bernard McGinn (ed.), *Meister Eckhart and the Beguine Mystics Hadewijch of Brabant, Mechthild of Magdeburg, and Marguerite Porete* (New York: Continuum, 1994) and Amy Hollywood, *The Soul as Virgin Wife: Mechthild of Magdeburg, Marguerite Porete and Meister Eckhart* (Notre Dame and London: University of Notre Dame Press, 1996). For Eckhart's teaching on nothingness, see Beverly J. Lanzetta, 'Three Categories of Nothingness in Eckhart', *The Journal of Religion* 72 (1992), 248–68.

4. Sermon 38 in the Stuttgart edition, No. 29 in Walshe's English translation (1987), Vol. I, p. 215. Hereafter, German texts will be cited as either DW for *Deutsche Werke* (Quint, 1936) or DP for *Deutsche Predigten* (Quint, 1955). Unless otherwise indicated, English citations will be taken from the translation by M. O'C. Walshe (1987). The sermon number in that edition will be abbreviated as W followed by the number of the sermon, volume, and page.

5. DW 5b, DP 6 (W 13b, I, 117).

6. DW 23 (W 54, II, 72).

7. DW 82, DP 54 (W 62, II, 115).

8. DW 9, DP 10 (W 67, II, 151). This statement was singled out for condemnation in Avignon as Proposition 28. Eckhart is simply pointing out that by the logic of the *via eminentiae*, God's attributes are substantial, whereas ours come and go and permit of comparative development. In a brilliant summary that must have dazzled his listeners, Eckhart said elsewhere, 'God is nameless because none can say or understand anything about Him. Concerning this a pagan master says that what we understand or declare about the first cause is more what we ourselves are than what the first cause is, because it is above all speech or understanding. If I now say God is good, it is not true; rather, I am good, God is not good. I will go further and say I am better than God for what is good can become better, and what can become better can become best of all. Now God is not good, therefore He cannot become better. And since He cannot become better, therefore He cannot become best; for these three, good, better and best, are remote from God, *since He is above them all.* Thus, too, if I say God is wise, it is not true: I am wiser than He. So too if I say God is a being, that is not true: *He is a transcendent being, and a superessential nothingness.*' (DW 83, DP 42 (W 96, II, 332–33), emphasis added). Cf. DW 12, DP 13 (W 57, II, 85); DW 69 (W 42, I, 293); DW 77 (W 49, II, 38–39); *Commentary in John*, Colledge-McGinn 1981, p. 128, etc.

10. DW 57 (W 26, I, 202). For a stimulating discussion of Eckhart's use of negative discourse, see Marius Buning, 'Negativity Then and Now: An Exploration of Meister Eckhart, Angelus Silesius and Jacques Derrida', *Eckhart Review* 4 (Spring 1995), 19–35.

11. DW 83, DP 42 (W 96, II, 333).

12. DP 58 (W 2, I, 20).
13. DP 59 (W 4, I, 40–1).
14. *On Detachment*, Walshe 1987, III, 292.
15. DW 52, DP 30 (W 87, II, 269–70).
16. DW 51, W 83, II, 254.
17. Eckhart refers to the divine cloud in terms of unknowing in DW 69 (W 42, I, 293) and DW 51, DP 24 (W 83, II, 254).
18. DP 57 (W 1, I, pp. 8–11). Eckhart continues, eventually linking the darkness of unknowing with the practice of radical detachment: 'Now you might say, "What does God do without images in the ground and essence?"

    'That I cannot know, because my soul's powers receive only in images; they have to know and lay hold of each thing in its appropriate image. They cannot recognize a horse when presented with the image of a man; and since all things enter from without, that knowledge is hidden from my soul – which is to her great advantage. This *not-knowing* makes her wonder and leads her to eager pursuit, for she perceives clearly *that* it is, but does not know *how* or *what* it is. Whenever a man knows the causes of things, then he at once tires of them and seeks to know something different. Always clamouring to know things, is for ever inconstant. And so this unknown knowing keeps the soul constant and yet spurs her on to pursuit. . . . Though it may be called a nescience, an unknowing, yet there is in it more than in all knowing and understanding without it, for this unknowing lures and attracts you from all understood things, and from yourself as well. This is what Christ meant when he said: "Whoever will not deny himself and will not leave his father and mother, and is not estranged from all these, is not worthy of me" (Matt. 10:37) . . .'
19. DW 86 (W 9, I, 83–85).
20. DP 57 (W 1, I, 8. Cf. DW 71, DP 37 (W 19, I, 158–9)): 'If we are to know God it must be without means, and then nothing alien can enter in. If we do see God in this light, it must be quite private and indrawn, without the intrusion of anything created. Then we have an immediate knowledge of eternal life.' Here, 'means' are conceptual tools, ideas, images, even sensory representations. See also *Talks of Instruction*, Colledge-McGinn 1981, 212.
21. DW 5b, DP 6 (W 13b, I, 117–18). Elsewhere, Eckhart says, 'We find people who like the taste of God in one way but not in another, and they want to have God only in one way of contemplation, not in another. I raise no objection, but they are quite wrong. If you want to take God properly, you should take Him equally in all things, in hardship as in comfort, in weeping as in joy, it should be all the same to you' (DW 5a, DP 5 (W13a, I, 112)).
22. Similarly, Eckhart taught his novices, 'He who has God thus essentially, takes Him divinely, and for him God shines forth in all things, for all things taste divinely to him, and God's image appears to him

from out of all things. God flashes forth in him always, in him there is detachment and turning away, and he bears the imprint of his beloved, present God' (*Talks of Instruction*, Walshe 1987, III, 18).

23. DW 68, DP 36 (W 69, II, 187). For a contemporary approach to God as rigorously apophatic and yet as delightfully 'ordinary' as Eckhart's way, see J. B. Phillips, *Your God Is Too Small* (New York: Macmillan, 1961).

24. Hinnebusch 1973, 322–3.

25. W 3, I, 28. Considered dubious despite parallels in both Latin and German sermons. Cf. Eckhart's remarks to his early disciples, ' . . . one must sometimes leave such a state of joy for a better one of love, and sometimes to perform a work of love where it is needed, whether it be spiritual or bodily. As I have said before, if a man were in an ecstasy as St Paul was (2 Cor. 12:2–4), and if he knew of a sick person who needed a bowl of soup from him, I would consider it far better if you were to leave that rapture out of love and help the needy person out of greater love' (*Talks of Instruction*, Walshe trans., III, 24–5).

26. In January, 1992, the panel's conclusions, *Eckardus Theutonicus, homo doctus et sanctus*, were published by the University of Fribourg under the direction of Professors P. H. Stirnimann and Rudi Imbach. A preliminary investigation of Eckhart's trial commissioned by the panel, *Der Prozess gegen Meister Eckhart* by Professor Winfried Trusen of Würzburg, had already been published in 1988.

27. Cited by Ursula Fleming in *Meister Eckhart: The Man from Whom God Hid Nothing*, p. xix. See also p. 156. See also Édouard-Henri Wéber OP, 'À propos de Maître Eckhart et de son procès', *Mémoire Dominicaine*, N. 2 (Printemps 1993) 135–7.

Chapter 6: CATHERINE OF SIENA: THE MYSTIC IN ACTION

1. New Haven: Yale University Press, 1952, p. 511.

2. Bell's analysis of Catherine's life and mission and that of other Italian mystics is found in his study, *Holy Anorexia*, where he writes, 'In the end she had committed the sin of vainglory and had starved herself to death. It had been her will, not His, that had triumphed all these years and that now lay vanquished' (Chicago: University of Chicago Press, 1985), pp. 52–3.

3. English translations of Catherine's works include Catherine of Siena, *The Dialogue*, tr. and ed. Suzanne Noffke OP (New York: Paulist Press, 1980); *The Letters*, ed. Suzanne Noffke OP, Vol. 1 (Binghamton: State University of New York Press, 1988); *The Prayers*, ed. and tr. Suzanne Noffke OP (New York: Paulist Press, 1983); *Catherine of Siena, Selected Spiritual Writings*, ed. and intro. by Mary O'Driscoll OP (Hyde Park, NY: New City Press, 1993). For recent and standard works on Catherine see Raymond of Capua, *The Life of Catherine of Siena*, tr. and ed. Conleth Kearns OP, forward by Mary Ann Fatula OP

(Washington: Dominicana, 1994); Giulana Cavallini, *Things Visible and Invisible: Images in the Spirituality of Catherine of Siena*, tr. Sr M. Jeremiah OP (New York: Alba House, 1996); Augusta Theodosia Drane, *History of St Catherine of Siena and Her Companions*, 2 vols. (London: Burns, Oates & Washbourne, 4th ed., 1914); Mary Ann Fatula OP, *Catherine of Siena's Way* (London: Darton, Longman and Todd / Wilmington, DE: Michael Glazier, 1987); Suzanne Noffke OP, *Catherine of Siena: Vision through a Distant Eye* (Collegeville, MN: Liturgical Press, 1996); Mary O'Driscoll OP, *Catherine of Siena* (Strasbourg: Éditions du Signe, 1994); and Arrigo Levasti, *My Servant, Catherine*, tr. D. M. White (Westminster, Md.: Newman, 1954).

4. Noffke 1996, p. 32, citing Raymond of Capua's *Life*, 11, n, 179–82, pp. 174–7.
5. Found in Drane 1914.
6. Letter 2, Cavallini 1996, 14. In referring to the Letters, I have followed the convention, where appropriate, of using T for the [Niccoló] Tommasèo edition (Berbera-Florence, 1860), and D for the [Eugenio] Dupré Theseider-Antonio Volpato edition (Rome, 1940).
7. Letter 52, Cavallini 1996, 30.
8. Noffke 1996, 40.
9. Noffke, *The Dialogue*, 'Introduction', p. 10.
10. Cited in Antonia Lacey, *The Symbolic Value of Gender: What Links Irigaray's Linguistic Theories and the Gender Specific Language and Female Imagery used by Catherine of Siena?* (unpublished MA diss., Brookes University, Oxford, October 1996), p. 16. The reference is to Carolyn Walker Bynum, *Holy Feast, Holy Fast: The Religious Significance of Food to Medieval Women* (Los Angeles: University of California Press, 1987), p. 178. On the symbolism of food in Catherine's writing, also see Cavallini 1996, 28–30.
11. Cavallini 1996, 55.
12. *Life*, I, x, 93, p. 86. Cited by Noffke 1996, 11.
13. Journet 1948, 7.
14. Cavallini 1996, 54–5.
15. Letter 246, cited in Cavallini 1996, 14.
16. DW 4, DP 4 (W 40, I, 284). The first part of this statement, which, taken as a whole, is conventionally orthodox, but not Thomistic, was condemned as Article 26. Cf. DW 69 (W 42, p. 293): 'All creatures God ever created or might yet create, if He wished, are little or nothing compared with God.'
17. Letter T68, to Bandeçça de' Belforti, cited by Noffke 1996, 11–12.
18. *The Dialogue* 1980, 43.
19. Letter 189, cited in Cavallini 1996, 15.
20. *The Dialogue* 1980, 164. Cited in Noffke 1996, 33.
21. Letter 226 to Raymond of Capua. Cited in O'Driscoll 1993, 36.
22. Letter 219. Cited in Cavallini 1996, 10–11.

23. Noffke 1996, 76. Hinnebusch remarks, similarly, of Catherine's unsuccessful campaigns toward the end of her life: 'Catherine's lack of diplomatic training and the gravity of the problems she tried to solve were responsible for her unimpressive record in public affairs. The problems taxed to the full the professional talents of the leaders of Christendom. Their efforts too, marked by mediocrity and weak motivation, were fruitless. Diplomacy was no more successful than prayer. Catherine's belief that the issues of her day could be solved by appealing to moral and spiritual motives may be considered naive when we look at the reality of the political and spiritual situation, yet she was correct in urging justice and charity as the true foundations of a lasting solution. She should be judged by the soundness of this evangelical outlook, not by the failure of others to act in accord with it' (Hinnebusch 1973, II, 355–9).

24. Cf. Letter T39, to Don Jacomo, a Carthusian of Pontignano. Cited in Noffke 1996, 77.

25. Letter T16 to a great prelate. Cited Fatula 1987, 72.

26. Letter T330 to Raymond of Capua. Cited Fatula 1987, 72, who comments, 'Catherine knew that her passion for truth mirrors the yearning deep in every human heart to live in clarity, not shadows, to live free and not as a slave. She knew that the same one who had bent down to her hunger for the truth desires to fill that hunger in every mind and heart regardless of how weak or inadequate: "And who am I that you give me your truth?... Your truth... does and accomplishes all things, because I am not. It is your truth that offers truth, and with your truth I speak the truth" [*Prayer* 21, Noffke ed., p. 193]'.

27. Fatula 1987, 192.

28. Letter 280 to Raymond, cited Fatula 1987, 193.

29. Bell writes, '... I assume, although it cannot be proved or disproved, that the onset of Saint Catherine of Siena's anorexia was a consequence not primarily of lesions in her hypothalamus but of psychic factors, in her case her will to conquer bodily urges that she considered base obstructions in her path of holiness. Once the pattern of conquest and reward was established, no doubt, acting through her hypothalamus, starvation intensified the consequences of her holy anorexia and ultimately she died in a state of inanition, or, as her confessor tells us, exhausted by her holy austerities' (Bell 1985, 15). *Anorexia nervosa* was not diagnosed as a medical illness until the latter part of the nineteenth century. To analyze Catherine's life and accomplishments dismissively on the assumption that, because of her admittedly complex relationship with food, eating, and the body in general, she was anorexic in the sense in which that term is used today, is not only reductionistic but as tendentious as the now-laughable efforts to exploit Freudian concepts in order to reduce (and dismiss) the ecstatic experiences of St Teresa of Ávila as the out-

growth of repressed infantile sexual urges concerning her father, as did James H. Leuba and his imitators in the early part of the century.

30. See in particular, Patricia O'Connell Killen, *Finding Our Voices: Women, Wisdom, and Faith* (New York: Crossroad, 1997).

31. Lacey 1997, 28.

Chapter 7: BEYOND THE WAYLESS WAY

1. Although the history of Thomism has been well documented, few studies have been devoted to the development of Thomas' spiritual influence. Hence the importance of the recent works by Ashley, Torrell, and Tugwell.

2. The interesting story of the association of the nuns and the preachers in a mutual enthusiasm for mystical spirituality and study has been told elsewhere. See *Margareta Ebner: Revelations and Pater Noster*, Leonard Hindsley OP and Margot Schmidt, eds. and intro., preface by Richard Woods OP (New York: Paulist Press, 1993); Woods 1987, and Hinnebusch 1966, I, 386–97.

3. For an exploration of this aspect of fourteenth-century Dominican life, see John Coakley, 'Friars as Confidants of Holy Women in Medieval Dominican Hagiography', in Blumenfeld-Kosinski and Szell 1991, pp. 222–46; Debra L. Stoudt, 'The Production and Preservation of Letters by Fourteenth-Century Dominican Nuns', *Medieval Studies* 53 (1991): 309–26; and André Vauchez, 'Lay People's Sanctity in Western Europe: Evolution of a Pattern (Twelfth and Thirteenth Centuries)', in Blumenfeld-Kosinski and Szell, ed. cit., pp. 21–32.

4. For a brief discussion of Nicholas' works, see Hinnebusch 1973, II, 302.

5. 'In the fourteenth and fifteenth centuries – as the large number of manuscripts proves – [*The Little Book of Eternal Wisdom*] was the most widely read spiritual book in Germany. It is considered to be the fairest fruit of German mysticism' (Martin, in Townsend 1934, 51).

6. Hinnebusch writes, 'Because Martin Luther admired and quoted him, Tauler was viewed with suspicion by sixteenth-century Catholics. John Eck, the leading Catholic polemicist, who had read Tauler superficially, charged him with heresy. During the second half of the century, the Spanish Inquisition put Pseudo-Tauler's *Divinae Institutiones* on the Index; Edward Mercurian, superior general of the Jesuits, forbade his subjects to read the works of Saints Gertrude and Mathilda [Mechthild], Raymond Lull, John Ruysbroeck, Henry Suso and John Tauler; and in 1594 the Capuchins of the province of Ghent issued a similar edict' (Hinnebusch 1973, II, 323).

7. Suso's life and works are treated in detail in Henry Suso, *The Exemplar, with Two German Sermons*, Frank Tobin, trans. and ed., preface by Bernard McGinn, New York: Paulist Press, 1989. See also

James M. Clark (trans.), *Henry Suso: Little Book of Eternal Wisdom and Little Book of Truth* (London: Faber, 1953); Henry Suso, *Wisdom's Watch upon the Hours*, trans. by Edmund Colledge OSA (Washington, DC: Catholic University of America Press, 1994); and *The Exemplar: Life and Writings of the Blessed Henry Suso, O.P.*, ed. by Nicholas Heller, trans. by Ann Edwards OP (Dubuque, IA: Priory Press, 1962).

8. Tobin 1989, 317–18.
9. Tobin 1989, 197.
10. Tobin 1989, 198. The power of Suso's language is well conveyed in Tobin's translation of the remainder of this section: 'In this wild mountain region of the "where" beyond God there is an abyss full of play and feeling for all pure spirits, and the spirit enters into this secret namelessness (of God) and into this wild, foreign terrain. This is a deep, bottomless abyss for all creatures and is intelligible to God alone. It is hidden for everything that is not God, except for those with whom he wants to share himself. And even these must seek him with detachment and in some manner must know as he knows.'
11. A sketch of Tauler's life and teachings by Joseph Schmidt is found in Johann Tauler, *Sermons*, trans. by Maria Shrady, intro. by Josef Schmidt, preface by Alois Haas (New York: Paulist Press, 1987). See also John Tauler, *Spiritual Conferences*, trans. and ed. by Eric Colledge and Sr Mary Jane Colledge OP (Rockford IL: TAN Books and Publishers, 1978); John Tauler, *The Sermons and Conferences*, trans. with intro. by Walter Elliot (Washington, DC, 1910); Susannah Winkworth (ed. and tr.), *The History and Life of the Reverend John Tauler, with Twenty-Five of His Sermons* (London: Allenson & Co., n.d.); and John Tauler, *Meditations on the Life and Passion of Our Lord Jesus Christ, attributed to John Tauler, Dominican Friar*, trans. by A. J. P. Cruikshank, pref. by Bertrand Wilberforce OP (London: Art and Book Co., 1904).
12. Sermon 11, Shrady 1987, 59. Less like Eckhart, Tauler goes on to explain, 'This "darkness" is to be understood in such a way: It is a light inaccessible to created reason, far beyond its comprehension. It is a wilderness because no natural path leads to it. In this wilderness the spirit is raised above itself, above all its powers of comprehension and understanding, and the soul now drinks from the very spring, from the true and essential source.'
13. Sermon 76, 22nd Sunday after Trinity, Shrady 1987, 172.
14. Hinnebusch 1973, II, 323.
15. The presence of themes such as the nothingness and incomprehensibility of God, spiritual poverty, and unknowing in Beguine circles prior to Eckhart, Suso, and Tauler, especially in the works of Marguerite Porete, Hadewijch of Antwerp, and Mechthild of Magdeburg, is the subject of several recent studies. See Amy Hollywood, *The Soul as Virgin Wife: Mechthild of Magdeburg, Marguerite Porete and Meister Eckhart* (Notre Dame and London: University of Notre Dame

Press, 1996), and Bernard McGinn (ed.), *Meister Eckhart and the Beguine Mystics Hadewijch of Brabant, Mechthild of Magdeburg, and Marguerite Porete* (New York: Continuum, 1994).

16. An extensive and critical account of Merswin's life and writings with a selection of writings is found in Thomas S. Kepler (ed.), *Mystical Writings of Rulman Merswin* (Philadelphia: Westminster, 1960).

17. Kepler 1960, 125.

18. Cf. Dom François Vanderbroucke, in *A History of Christian Spirituality* (London: Burns and Oates, 1968), Vol. II, 398. For an excellent translation and detailed introduction, see C. F. Kelley (ed.), *The Book of the Poor in Spirit by a Friend of God* (New York: Harper and Brothers, 1954).

19. Kelley 1954, 41–2.

20. Kelley 1954, 104.

21. Kelley 1954, 166.

22. Kelley 1954, 178–9.

23. A copy of the text made in 1497 and discovered in the last century seems to be closer to the original than the version edited by Luther in 1516 and 1518. See *The Theologia Germanica of Martin Luther*, trans. by Bengt Hoffman (New York: Paulist Press, 1980). One still finds copies of an older if less reliable translation by Susannah Winkworth from 1854 (London: Macmillan, 1901).

24. Ch. 53, in Winkworth 1901, 212–14, text slightly modernized.

25. Several good translations of *The Cloud of Unknowing* exist by Hodgson, Johnston, Wolters, and others. Closest to the Middle English version is *The Cloud Of Unknowing and Other Treatises by an English Mystic of the Fourteenth Century, with a Commentary on The Cloud by Father Augustine Baker O.S.B.*, edited by Abbot Justin McCann OSB (Westminster, Maryland: The Newman Press, 1952). For the critical text see *The Cloud Of Unknowing and Related Treatises*, ed. by Phyllis Hodgson (Salzburg: Institut Für Anglistik und Amerikanistik Universität) (Analecta Cartusiana, general ed. Dr James Hogg, 1982. An accurate modern translation with extensive notes can be found in James A. Walsh SJ ed. and intro., *The Cloud of Unknowing*, preface by Simon Tugwell OP (New York: Paulist Press, 1981). For commentary, see Turner 1995 and Marion Glasscoe, *English Medieval Mystics: Games of Faith* (London and NY: Longman, 1993).

26. Cf. Dom David Knowles, *The English Mystical Tradition* (New York: Harper, 1961), pp. 36–8, 74–7, 95–6. For the author as a (former) Dominican, see esp. p. 71. However, as there were Dominican hermits in fourteenth-century England, there is no compelling reason to assume that the author was an ex-Dominican simply because he was a solitary. And, as Maurice Walshe, Eckhart's major English translator of our time, has said, 'It is remarkable that the introduction [to McCann's edition] mentions Tauler, Suso, Ruysbroeck and St

Catherine of Siena as 14th century contemplatives, but not Eckhart! There are of course many parallels to Eckhart's thought in *The Cloud of Unknowing*' (Walshe 1987, I, 13).

27. I have slightly modernized McCann's reading of this and the following citations.

28. English versions include John Ruusbroec, *The Spiritual Espousals and Other Works*, intro. and trans. by James Wiseman OSB, preface by Louis Dupré (New York: Paulist Press, 1985) and Jan van Ruysbroeck, *The Seven Steps of the Ladder of Spiritual Love*, trans. by F. Sherwood Taylor (Westminster: Dacre Press, 1943). For commentary, see the valuable introduction by James Wiseman in the 1985 edition and Louis Dupré, *The Common Life: The Origins of Trinitarian Mysticism and Its Development by Jan Ruusbroec* (New York: Crossroad, 1984).

29. Wiseman 1985, 100.

30. III, 1, cited by Wiseman 1985, 32.

31. Texts include Nicholas Cusanus, *On Learned Ignorance*, trans. by Germanus Heron OFM (London: Routledge and Kegan Paul, 1954); Nicholas of Cusa, *The Vision of God*, trans. by Emma Gurney Salter (London and New York: J. M. Dent and E. P. Dutton, 1928). See also Jasper Hopkins (trans. and ed.), *Nicholas of Cusa's Debate with John Wenck: A Translation and an Appraisal of De Ignota Litteratura and Apologia Doctae Ignorantiae* (Minneapolis: A. J. Banning, 1981) and Jasper Hopkins (trans. and ed.), *Nicholas of Cusa's Dialectical Mysticism: Text, Translation and Interpretative Study of De Visione Dei* (Minneapolis: A. J. Banning, 1985).

32. Donald F. Duclow, 'Mystical Theology and Intellect in Nicholas of Cusa', *American Catholic Philosophical Quarterly* LXIV, 1 (Winter 1990): 127.

Chapter 8: IN THE END, GOD

1. On the dispute regarding the authorship of the Dionysian works, see Karlfried Froelich, 'Pseudo-Dionysius and the Reformation of the Sixteenth Century', in Luibheid 1987, pp. 38–46.

2. Ashley 1990, 60. He adds, 'Hence Raymond's reform, though it saved the Order, also had some unhappy consequences. "Monastic observance" came to overshadow St Dominic's single-minded goal of an Order of Preachers. Also the government of the Order became more centralized in order to empower the Master to defend the "Observants" against the hostility of General Chapters elected by "conventual" majorities. Hence after 1370 Chapters met not annually but only every two or three years. Finally, the Conventuals remained the majority in many provinces and their dislike of the Observants made for constant faction and friction. Fortunately, unlike the Franci-

scans, Carmelites, and others, the Dominicans never split into separate orders' (Ashley 1990, 60–1).

3. On the life, work, and accomplishments of Fra Angelico (1400–55), see Thomas McGonigle OP and Gail Geiger, *Art and Spirituality in Fifteenth-Century Florence* (Cambridge: Cambridge University Press, 1998); Guy Bedouelle OP, *In the Image of St Dominic: Nine Portraits of Dominican Life*, tr. Sr Mary Thomas Noble (San Francisco: Ignatius Press, 1994); and John Pope-Hennessy, *Fra Angelico* (Ithaca, NY: Cornell University Press, 2nd ed., 1974).

4. For a still absorbing view of Vincent's life and work, see Henry Gheon, *St Vincent Ferrer* (New York: Sheed and Ward, 1954). Works in English include *A Treatise On The Spiritual Life*, with a commentary by Mother Julienne Morrell (Westminster, MD: Newman Press, 1951 / London, Blackfriars Publications, 1957).

5. Ed. cit. 1957, 'On Purity of Heart', 64.

6. Ironically, the commentary on his little volume on spiritual perfection by Mother Julienne Morrell in the sixteenth century is in many respects more interesting and probably a more reliable spiritual guide today than Vincent's own work.

7. Ed. cit. 1957, 92–3.

8. Texts and sources include *The Compendium of Revelations* in *Apocalyptic Spirituality: Treatises and Letters of Lactantius, Adso of Montier-en-Der, Joachim of Fiore, the Franciscan Spirituals, Savonarola*, ed. and intro. by Bernard McGinn (New York: Paulist Press, 1979), pp. 192–276; *The Triumph of the Cross*, ed. and intro. by John Proctor (London: Sands and Co., 1901); Michael de la Bedoyere, *The Meddlesome Friar: the Story of the Conflict between Savonarola and Alexander VI* (London: Collins, 1957); Pierre Van Paassen, *A Crown of Fire: the Life and Times of Girolamo Savonarola* (London: Hutchinson, 1961); Roberto Ridolfi, *The Life of Girolamo Savonarola*, tr. Cecil Grayson (London; Alfred A. Knopf, Inc., 1959); and Donald Weinstein, *Savonarola and Florence: Prophecy and Patriotism in the Renaissance* (Princeton: Princeton University Press, 1970).

9. Bedouelle 1994, 85.

10. The most recent work on Las Cases is the massive study by Gustavo Gutiérrez, *Las Casas: In Search of the Poor of Jesus Christ*, tr. Robert R. Barr (New York: Orbis, 1993). For an insightful study of the prophetic and mystical achievements of St Martin de Porres, see Alex García-Rivera, *St Martín de Porres: The 'Little Stories' and the Semiotics of Culture*, foreword by Virgil Elizondo, intro. by Robert Schreiter (Maryknoll, NY: Orbis Press, 1996).

11. See St Catherine de' Ricci, *Selected Letters*, ed., selected and introduced by Dominico Di Agresti, tr. Jennifer Petrie (Oxford: Dominican Sources in English, 1985).

12. For an anthology of outstanding Dominican figures, lavishly illustrated with works by contemporary artists, see Austin Flannery OP

(ed.), *Saint Dominic and His Family* (Dublin: Dominican Publications, 1998).

13. Portions of this section were published in *Presence*, Sept. 1997.

14. Karen Armstrong, *A History of God* (New York: Alfred Knopf, 1994), p. xvii.

15. See, e.g., Elizabeth Johnson, *She Who Is: The Mystery of God in Feminist Discourse* (New York: Crossroad, 1992); Sallie McFague, *Models of God* (Philadelphia: Fortress Press, 1987).

16. Jack Miles, *God: A Biography* (New York: Random House, 1995).

17. For a modern restatement of the need for a liberating de-conceptualization of God, see J. B. Phillip's superb little classic, *Your God Is Too Small* (New York: Macmillan, 1961.)

18. DW 52 (W 87, II, 271). I have removed the quotation marks that Prof. Walshe, like many translators, inserts around 'God' to protect Eckhart's orthodoxy, something Eckhart would have found unnecessary and misleading.

19. Ibid., p. 275.

20. Commenting on these passages, the contemporary German theologian, Jürgen Moltmann writes, 'The breaking of the shell, so as to reach the kernel; the abolition of the mediations, so as to arrive at the goal; the step by step withdrawal of created things, revelations and divine condescensions, so that God may be loved for himself; and then the abolition of God for God's sake – these are the ultimate possibilities of the mystical journey which are expressible at all' (Jürgen Moltmann, *The Spirit of Life: A Universal Affirmation*, tr. Margaret Kohl (Minneapolis: Augsburg Fortress Press/London: SCM Press, 1992), p. 207).

21. Moltmann 1992, 208.

BIBLIOGRAPHY

There are very helpful bibliographies of older and recent works in English in Benedict Ashley OP, *The Dominicans* and *Spiritual Direction in the Dominican Tradition* (see below). With regard to more specialist areas, particularly in the medieval tradition, extensive bibliographies can be found in the books by Tugwell, McGinn, and Noffke. The following works represent a basic list of reference works, some of which are listed in the books just named. I have also included works that were published afterwards or which are useful sources in regard to subjects in this volume.

I GENERAL

Ashley, Benedict, OP, *The Dominicans* (Collegeville, MN: Liturgical Press, 1990). An excellent brief history of the Dominican Order. Similar to the short history by Hinnebusch, it is fuller and more accessible as well as up-to-date.

Spiritual Direction in the Dominican Tradition (New York: Paulist Press, 1995).

Bedouelle, Guy, OP, *In the Image of St Dominic: Nine Portraits of Dominican Life*, tr. Sr Mary Thomas Noble (San Francisco: Ignatius Press, 1994). Fine short essays on nine Dominican saints and saintly figures: Jordan of Saxony, Peter of Verona, Thomas Aquinas, Catherine of Siena, Fra Angelico (John of Fiesole), Bartolomé de las Casas, Catherine de' Ricci, Martin de Porres, and Henri Lacordaire. Short excerpts from their writings or about them are included. Although popular rather than academic in intent, the essays are carefully researched and annotated.

Blumenfeld-Kosinski, Renate and Szell, Timea (eds.), *Images of Sainthood in Medieval Europe* (Ithaca and London: Cornell University Press, 1991). A valuable collection of essays about medieval spirituality, including an excellent discussion of Dominican spiritual direction of Beguines by John Coakley.

Flannery, Austin, OP (ed.), *Saint Dominic and His Family* (Dublin: Dominican Publications, 1998). A wonderfully illustrated collection of brief lives of Dominic and outstanding representatives of the Order of Preachers.

Gardeil, Ambroise, OP, *The Gifts of the Holy Ghost in Dominican Saints* (Milwaukee: Bruce, 1937).

Garrigou-Lagrange, Reginald, OP, 'Character and Principles of Dominican Spirituality' in Townsend, pp. 57–82.

Hinnebusch, William A., OP, *The Dominicans. A Short History* (New York: Alba House, 1975).

   Dominican Spirituality: Principles and Practices (Washington, DC: The Thomist Press, 1965). Somewhat dated, but still an important source for understanding Dominican spirituality up to the Second Vatican Council.

   The History of the Dominican Order, 2 vols. (Staten Island, NY: Alba House, 1966 and 1973). A classic and indispensable work by the late Dominican historian which traces the history of the Order from its beginnings to 1500.

Jarrett, Bede, OP, *The English Dominicans* (London, 1921). A classic work by one of the outstanding Dominicans of the century.

Journet, Charles, *The Dark Knowledge of God*, tr. James F. Anderson (London: Sheed and Ward, 1948). A small gem of a work which summarizes the main lines of Christian apophatic theology.

Little, Lester K., *Religious Poverty and the Profit Economy in the Middle Ages* (Ithaca: Cornell University Press, 1978). Contains excellent material on the historical context of the early Order.

Lossky, Vladimir, *The Mystical Theology of the Eastern Church* (Cambridge and London: James Clarke and Co., 1957). An important source for understanding the development of the spirituality of the early Church.

   The Vision of God, tr. Asheleigh Moorhouse, preface by John Meyendorff (Bedfordshire: The Faith Press, 1963).

Louth, Andrew, *Denys the Areopagite* (London: Geoffrey Chapman/ Wilton, CT: Morehouse Barlow, 1989).

   The Origins of the Christian Mystical Tradition (Oxford: Clarendon Press, 1981).

Martin, Raymond M., OP, 'The Historical Development of Dominican Spirituality' in Townsend, pp. 27–55.

Ruusbroec, John, *The Spiritual Espousals and Other Works*, intro. and tr. James Wiseman OSB, preface by Louis Dupré (New York: Paulist Press, 1985).

Schillebeeckx, Edward, OP, 'Dominican Spirituality, or The Counter-Thread in the Old Religious Story as the Golden Thread in the Dominican Family-Story', *Dominican Topics in South Africa*, March, May, and August, 1975.

Sells, Michael A., *Mystical Languages of Unsaying* (Chicago: University of Chicago Press, 1994). A recent and important work on apophatic theology.

Terrien, Samuel, *The Elusive Presence* (San Francisco: Harper and Row, 1978). A profound and seminal biblical study of the 'hiddenness' of God.

Townsend, Anselm, OP (ed. and tr.), *Dominican Spirituality* (Milwaukee: Bruce Publishing Co., 1934). Translation of *La vie spirituelle* 4 (Aug. 1921). Excellent articles from early in this century by French Dominicans including Petitot, Martin, Garrigou-Lagrange, Bernadot, Cathala.

Tugwell, Simon, OP, *The Way of the Preacher* (London: Darton, Longman and Todd, 1979).

Ways of Imperfection (Springfield, IL: Templegate, 1985).

Woods, Richard, OP, *Christian Spirituality: God's Presence through the Ages* (Allen, TX: Thomas More, 1996). A single-volume handbook detailing the origin, development, and history of Christian spirituality from New Testament times to the present.

II THE EARLY DOMINICANS

Texts:

Early Dominicans: Selected Writings, ed. Simon Tugwell OP (New York: Paulist Press, 1982).

Koudelka, Vladimir, OP, *Dominic*, ed. and tr. Simon Tugwell OP (London: Darton, Longman and Todd, 1997).

Commentaries:

Bedouelle, Guy, OP, *Saint Dominic. The Grace of the Word* (San Francisco: Ignatius Press, 1987).

Bennett, R. F., *The Early Dominicans: Studies in Thirteenth-Century Dominican History* (Cambridge: The University Press, 1937). An older but still very readable and excellent study of the early Order.

d'Avray, D. L., *The Preaching of the Friars: Sermons Diffused from Paris before 1300* (Oxford: Clarendon Press, 1985). An essential resource for serious study of the origins and early history of mendicant preaching. Although restricted to the thirteenth century, d'Avray provides valuable information on later periods.

Tugwell, Simon, OP, *Saint Dominic* (Strasbourg: Éditions du Signe, 1995). A superb and beautifully illustrated booklet by a major historian of the Order.

Vicaire, M.-H., OP, *Saint Dominic and His Times*, tr. Kathleen Ponds (Green Bay, WI: ALT Publishing Co., 1964).

The Genius of Saint Dominic, A Collection of Study-Essays (Nagpur, India: Dominican Publications, 1981).

Weisheipl, James, OP (ed.), *Albertus Magnus and the Sciences, Commemorative Essays* (Toronto: Pontifical Institute of Medieval Studies, 1980).

III ST THOMAS AQUINAS

Texts:

St Thomas Aquinas, *Faith, Reason and Theology, Questions I-IV of his Commentary on the De Trinitate of Boethius,* tr. with intro. and notes by Armand Maurer (Toronto: Pontifical Institute of Mediaeval Studies, 1987).

Thomas Aquinas: The Gifts of the Spirit – Selected Spiritual Writings, ed. and intro. Benedict Ashley OP, tr. Matthew Rzeczkowski OP (Hyde Park, NY: New City Press, 1996).

Albert and Thomas: Selected Writings, ed. and intro. Simon Tugwell OP (New York: Paulist Press, 1988).

Commentaries:

Barron, Robert, *Thomas Aquinas: Spiritual Master* (New York: Crossroad, 1996). A recent and very readable presentation of Thomas as a spiritual writer based on his teaching as a whole.

Chenu, M.-D., OP, *Towards Understanding St Thomas,* tr. Albert Landry OP and Dominic Hughes OP (Chicago: Henry Regnery, 1963). Essential work of historical exegesis regarding the development of Thomas' thought.

Davies, Brian, OP, *The Thought of Thomas Aquinas* (Oxford and New York: Clarendon Press, 1992). An excellent overview of the philosophical and theological teaching of Thomas.

Fatula, Mary Ann, OP, *Thomas Aquinas: Preacher and Friend* (Collegeville, MN: Liturgical Press, 1993).

Fox, Matthew, *Sheer Joy* (San Francisco: HarperCollins, 1992). A weighty collection of excerpts from Thomas' works arranged in an innovative dialogue between the Angelic Doctor and the acknowledged leader of the 'creation spirituality' movement.

Grabmann, Martin, *The Interior Life of Thomas Aquinas,* tr. Nicholas Ashenbrenner (Milwaukee: Bruce Publishing Co., 1951).

Hankey, W. J., *God in Himself: Aquinas' Doctrine of God as Expounded in the Summa Theologiae* (Oxford University Press, 1987). Contains important insights on the Neoplatonic element in St Thomas' thought.

McNabb, Vincent, 'The Mysticism of St Thomas Aquinas' in *Thomas Aquinas,* ed. Alfred Whitacre (St Louis: B. Herder Book Co., 1925).

O'Meara, Thomas F., OP, *Thomas Aquinas, Theologian* (Notre Dame: University of Notre Dame Press, 1997). A very recent work by an outstanding contemporary historian and theologian.

Petitot, Hyacinthe, *The Life and Spirit of Thomas Aquinas*, tr. Cyprian Burke (Chicago: Priory Press, 1966).

Pieper, Josef, *The Silence of St Thomas*, tr. John Murray sj and Daniel O'Connor (Chicago: Henry Regnery, 1965). Superb short work on Thomas, with an emphasis on his negative theology.

Principe, Walter H., *Thomas Aquinas' Spirituality*, Étienne Gilson Series, No. 7 (Toronto: Pontifical Institute of Medieval Studies, 1984).

Torrell, Jean-Pierre, op, *Saint Thomas Aquinas*, Volume I: The Person and His Work, tr. Robert Royal (Washington, DC, The Catholic University of America Press, 1996). First of two-part work under translation. Volume Two will concern Thomas' spiritual writings.

Weisheipl, James A., op, *Friar Thomas D'Aquino: His Life, Thought, and Works* (Washington, DC: The Catholic University of America Press, rev. ed., 1983). Definitive biography of Thomas with a good if somewhat dated bibliography of English translations.

IV   MEISTER ECKHART AND HIS CIRCLE

Texts:

Meister Eckhart: The Essential Sermons, Commentaries, Treatises and Defense, tr. and intro. by Edmund Colledge and Bernard McGinn (New York: Paulist Press, 1981).

Meister Eckhart: Selected Writings, tr. and ed. Oliver Davies (London: Penguin, 1994).

Meister Eckhart: Teacher and Preacher, ed. and tr. Bernard McGinn with Frank Tobin and Elvira Borgstädt, preface by Kenneth Northcott (New York: Paulist Press / London: SPCK, 1987).

Meister Eckhart, Sermons and Treatises, tr. M. O'C. Walshe, 3 vols. (Longmead, Shaftesbury, Dorset: Element Books, 1987).

Kelley, C. F. (ed. and tr.), *The Book of the Poor in Spirit by a Friend of God* (New York: Harper and Brothers, 1954). A good translation of an anonymous Rhineland mystical treatise once attributed to Johann Tauler.

Kepler, Thomas S. (ed.), *Mystical Writings of Rulman Merswin* (Philadelphia: Westminster, 1960). A good translation of the controversial writings of an important if eccentric mystic in the Rhineland tradition.

Margareta Ebner: Revelations and Pater Noster, ed. and intro. Leonard Hindsley op and Margot Schmidt, preface by Richard Woods op (New York: Paulist Press, 1993).

Mechthild von Magdeburg: *Flowing Light of the Divinity*, tr. Christiane Mesch Galvani (New York: Garland, 1991).

The Revelations of Mechthild of Magdeburg or The Flowing Light of the Godhead, tr. Lucy Menzies (London: Longmans, Green and Co., 1953 [not complete]).

Pickett, Brian, *The Heart of Love: Prayers of German Women Mystics* (Slough: St Paul Publications, 1991). A collection of prayers taken from the works of Dorothea of Montau, Elsbet Stagel, Elizabeth of Schönau, Gertrude of Hackeborn, Gertrude the Great, Hildegard of Bingen, Margaret Ebner, Mechthild of Hackeborn, Mechthild of Magdeburg, and Roswitha of Gandersheim.

Clark, James M. (tr.), *Henry Suso: Little Book of Eternal Wisdom and Little Book of Truth* (London: Faber, 1953).

Suso, Henry, *The Exemplar, with Two German Sermons*, tr. and ed. Frank Tobin, preface by Bernard McGinn (New York: Paulist Press, 1989).

Wisdom's Watch upon the Hours, tr. Edmund Colledge OSA (The Fathers of the Church, Mediaeval Continuation, Vol. 4), (Washington, DC: Catholic University of America Press, 1994). Translation of the *Horologium Sapientiae* with excellent introduction and notes.

Bizet, J. A., *Jean Tauler de Strasbourg* (Paris: Desclée, 1968). Valuable introduction and eight sermons in French translation.

Johann Tauler's Predigten auf alle Sonn- und Festage im Jahr, heraus. von Joh. Arndt und Phil. Jar. Spener, neue heraus. von Kuntze und Biesenthal, Berlin: Verlag von August von Hirschwald, 1841. 41 sermons in modern German translation of early nineteenth century.

Tauler, John, *Meditations on the Life and Passion of Our Lord Jesus Christ, attributed to John Tauler, Dominican Friar*, tr. by A. J. P. Cruikshank, preface by Bertrand Wilberforce OP (London: Art and Book Co., 1904).

Sermons, tr. Maria Shrady, intro. by Josef Schmidt, preface by Alois Haas (New York: Paulist Press, 1987).

Spiritual Conferences, tr. and ed. Eric Colledge and Sr Mary Jane Colledge OP (Rockford IL: TAN Books and Publishers, 1978).

The Sermons and Conferences, tr., with intro. by Walter Elliot (Washington, DC, 1910). A huge but serviceable compilation based on the German edition of 1864 with an eye to Surius' Latin version of 1553, containing some doubtful material and lacking critical apparatus.

Winkworth, Susannah (ed. and tr.), *The History and Life of the Reverend John Tauler, with Twenty-Five of His Sermons* (London: Allenson & Co., n.d.). Antique in concept and content.

Commentaries:

Colledge, Edmund, OSA, and. Marler, J. C., '"Mystical" Pictures in the Suso "Exemplar", *MS Strasbourg 2929*', *Archivum Fratrum Praedicatorum* 54 (1984): 293–354.

Davies, Oliver, *Meister Eckhart: Mystical Theologian* (London: SPCK, 1991).

Forman, Robert K., *Meister Eckhart: Mystic as Theologian* (Rockport, Mass./Shaftesbury, Dorset: Element Books, 1991).

Gieraths, Gundalf, OP, *Life in Abundance: Meister Eckhart and the German Dominican Mystics of the 14th Century, Spirituality Today Supplement*, Autumn, 1986.

Haas, Alois Maria, 'Schools of Late Medieval Mysticism', in Jill Raitt (ed.), *Christian Spirituality* (London: Routledge, 1987), pp. 140–75.

Hollywood, Amy, *The Soul as Virgin Wife: Mechthild of Magdeburg, Marguerite Porete and Meister Eckhart* (Notre Dame and London: University of Notre Dame Press, 1996).

Jones, Rufus, *The Flowering of Mysticism in the Fourteenth Century* (New York: Hafner Publishing Co., 1971, facsimile of 1939 ed.).

McGinn, Bernard (ed.), *Meister Eckhart and the Beguine Mystics Hadewijch of Brabant, Mechthild of Magdeburg, and Marguerite Porete* (New York: Continuum, 1994).

Smith, Dom Cyprian, OSB, *Meister Eckhart: The Way of Paradox* (London: Darton, Longman and Todd, 1988).

Tobin, Frank, *Mechthild von Magdeburg: A Medieval Mystic in Modern Eyes* (Columbia, SC: Camden House, 1995).

Turner, Denys, *The Darkness of God: Negativity in Christian Mysticism* (Cambridge: Cambridge University Press, 1995). Fine philosophical essays on Eckhart and his milieu and the larger tradition of apophatic theology.

Woods, Richard, OP, *Eckhart's Way* (London: Darton, Longman and Todd, 1987/Collegeville, MN: Liturgical Press, 1991).

' "I am the Son of God": Eckhart and Aquinas on the Incarnation', *Eckhart Review*, June 1992, pp. 27–46.

Vauchez, André, 'Lay People's Sanctity in Western Europe: Evolution of a Pattern (Twelfth and Thirteenth Centuries)', in Blumenfeld-Kosinski and Szell, ed. cit., pp. 21–32. Vauchez discusses the relationship between Dominican friars and holy women who were under their spiritual guidance and with whom they formed strong, sometimes emotionally dependent friendships.

Ziegler, Joanna, *Sculpture of Compassion: The Pieta and the Beguines in the Southern Low Countries c. 1300–c. 1600* (Brussels: Belgisch Historisch Institut te Rome, 1992).

V CATHERINE

Texts:

Catherine of Siena, *The Dialogue of Catherine of Siena*, tr. and ed. Suzanne Noffke OP (New York: Paulist Press, 1980).

The Letters, ed. Suzanne Noffke OP, Vol. 1 (Binghamton: State University of New York Press, 1988). (Volumes 2–4 and the revised Vol. 1 will be published by the State University of Arizona Press beginning in 1998.)

The Prayers, ed. and tr. Suzanne Noffke (New York: Paulist Press, 1983).

Catherine of Siena, Selected Spiritual Writings, ed. and intro. by Mary O'Driscoll OP (Hyde Park, NY: New City Press, 1993).

Raymond of Capua, *The Life of Catherine of Siena*, tr. and ed. Conleth Kearns OP, forward by Mary Ann Fatula OP (Washington: Dominicana, 1994 (1980)).

Commentaries:

Bynum, Carolyn Walker, *Holy Feast, Holy Fast: The Religious Significance of Food to Medieval Women* (Los Angeles: University of California Press, 1987).

Cavallini, Giuliana, *Things Visible and Invisible: Images in the Spirituality of Catherine of Siena*, tr. Sr M. Jeremiah OP (New York: Alba House, 1996).

Coakley, John, 'Friars as Confidants of Holy Women in Medieval Dominican Hagiography', in Blumenfeld-Kosinski and Szell, pp. 222–46.

Drane, Augusta Theodosia, *History of St Catherine of Siena and Her Companions*, 2 vols. (London: Burns, Oates & Washbourne, 4th ed., 1914).

Fatula, Mary Ann, OP, *Catherine of Siena's Way* (London: Darton, Longman and Todd/Wilmington, DE: Michael Glazier, 1987).

Levasti, Arrigo, *My Servant, Catherine*, tr. D. M. White (Westminster, Md.: Newman, 1954).

Noffke, Suzanne, OP, *Catherine of Siena: Vision through a Distant Eye* (Collegeville, MN: Liturgical Press, 1996).

O'Driscoll, Mary, OP, *Catherine of Siena* (Strasbourg: Éditions du Signe, 1994 (booklet)).

VI LATER DOMINICANS

García-Rivera, Alex, *St Martín de Porres: The "Little Stories" and the Semiotics of Culture*, foreword by Virgil Elizondo, intro. by Robert Schreiter (Maryknoll, NY: Orbis Press, 1996).

Gheon, Henry, *St Vincent Ferrer* (New York: Sheed and Ward, 1954).

Gutiérrez, Gustavo, *Las Casas: In Search of the Poor of Jesus Christ*, tr. Robert R. Barr (New York: Orbis, 1993).

McGonigle, Thomas, OP and Geiger, Gail, *Art and Spirituality in Fifteenth-Century Florence* (Cambridge: Cambridge University Press, 1998).

Pope-Hennessy, John, *Fra Angelico* (Ithaca, NY: Cornell University Press, 2nd ed. 1974).

Ridolfi, Roberto, *The Life of Girolamo Savonarola*, tr. Cecil Grayson (New York: Kuopf, 1959).

Rose Hawthorne Lathrop: Selected Writings, ed. Diana Culbertson OP (New York: Paulist Press, 1993).

Saint Vincent Ferrer OP, *A Treatise On The Spiritual Life*, with a commentary by Ven. Mother Julienne Morrell OP, tr. the Dominican Nuns, Corpus Christi Monastery, Menlo Park (California, Westminster, MD: Newman Press, 1951/London, Blackfriars Publications, 1957).

Savonarola, Girolamo, *The Compendium of Revelations in Apocalyptic Spirituality: Treatises and Letters of Lactantius, Adso of Montier-en-Der, Joachim of Fiore, the Franciscan Spirituals, Savonarola*, ed. and intro. by Bernard McGinn (New York: Paulist Press, 1979), pp. 192–276.

Wilms, Jerome, *Lay Brother, Artist and Saint (Bl. James of Ulm)*, tr. Sr M. Fulgence (London: Blackfriars, 1957).

VII RECENT AND CONTEMPORARY DOMINICANS

Arintero, Juan, OP, *The Mystical Evolution in the Development and Vitality of the Church*, 2 vols. (St Louis: B. Herder, 1949).

Bailey, Bede, OP, and Tugwell, Simon, OP (eds.), *Letters of Bede Jarrett* (Downside Abbey and Blackfriars Publications, 1989).

Jarrett, Bede, OP, *An Anthology of Bede Jarrett*, ed. Jordan Aumann (Dubuque, IA: Priory Press, 1961).

White, Allan, OP, 'Father Bede Jarrett, O.P., and The Renewal of the English Dominican Province', in Dominic Aidan Bellenger (ed.), *Opening the Scrolls. Essays in Honour of Godfrey Anstruther, O.P.* (Downside Abbey, 1987), pp. 216–84.

Wykeham-George Kenneth and Mathew, Gervase, *Bede Jarrett of the Order of Preachers* (London, 1952).

O'Meara, Thomas, OP, ' "Raid on the Dominicans": The Repression of 1954', *America*, 170, 4 (5 Feb. 1994): 8–16.

White, Victor, OP, *God and the Unconscious*, foreword by C. G. Jung (Dallas: Spring Publications, 1982 /London: The Harvill Press, 1952).
God the Unknown (London: The Harvill Press, 1956).
Soul and Psyche (London: Collins and Harvill, 1960).